THE TALMUD
FOR BEGINNERS

THE TALMUD FOR BEGINNERS

Volume 1
Prayer

Judith Z. Abrams

JASON ARONSON INC.
Northvale, New Jersey
London

Copyright © 1993 by Judith Z. Abrams

10 9 8 7 6 5 4 3 2 1

Library of Congress Cataloging-in-Publication Data

Abrams, Judith Z.
    The Talmud for beginners.

    Includes bibliographical references (p. 195–198) and indexes.
        Contents: v. 1. Prayer — v. 2. Text.
        1. Talmud—Introductions. I. Title.
BM503.5.A27 1991   296.1'2061   90-1211
ISBN 0-87668-734-6 (set)
ISBN 0-87668-719-2 (v. 1) (hb)
ISBN 1-56821-022-1 (v. 1) (pb)
ISBN 0-87668-597-1 (v. 2) (pb)

Manufactured in the United States of America. Jason Aronson Inc. offers books and cassettes. For information and catalog write to Jason Aronson Inc., 230 Livingston Street, Northvale, New Jersey 07647.

For Steven and Michael, with love

"How do women earn merit? By helping their families study."
Berachot 17a

Contents

Preface

One day, when I was 18 years old and facing the difficulties of becoming an adult, I needed to put my problems into perspective. I happened to be in a Jewish Community Center at the time, so I went into the library to look for some guidance. There, among the shelves of brightly bound books and periodicals, I saw a set of tomes bound in burgundy—imposing, stately, obviously a treasure trove of eternal truths. It was the Talmud, translated into English. I knew from my religious school classes that the Talmud held the wisdom of the ages and had been studied lovingly by our people for hundreds and hundreds of years. Here was what I was looking for: a font of wisdom, waiting to be drunk from like a can of soda.

I picked a volume from the middle of the row, eagerly opened it, and read, "When do turtle doves first become qualified for sacrifice? When their wing plumage becomes golden. And when do pigeons become disqualified? When their neck feathers begin to glisten"(*Hullin* 22b). I remember this moment so clearly that I was able to find the passage again after all these years. And I clearly remember my reaction, too. I thought, *This* is eternal wisdom? *This* is supposed to help me with my problems? *This* is what our people treasured for centuries? *Forget this!*

It was not until years later, when I started to study Talmud on a daily basis, that I began to understand its appeal. Eventually I realized that each volume, or tractate, of the Talmud is organized along specific patterns. Once learned, these patterns render the text comprehensible. And once you understand the

Talmud, you can see how glorious and meaningful it is. There is a reason that people have been studying it for centuries.

The rabbis are like a group of people who are working on a 5,000-piece jigsaw puzzle of incomparable beauty. They begin to piece the picture together bit by small bit. Some parts of the picture appear to be a cityscape; other parts portray the countryside. Some pieces are black as night; others are as blue as a summer sky. As the rabbis piece the puzzle together, they come closer and closer to understanding what the total picture looks like. They also treasure the experience of working together, the process of putting the pieces in their places and slowly discovering what the picture is about. This is the nature of Talmud study: The rabbis rarely tell you the bottom line. Instead, they take you through the process and let you figure it out for yourself. And as you do so, you add your own pieces to the picture and thereby make it, in some ways, your own.

This book is designed for two groups of readers. For the first, the lay reader who is not yet familiar with Talmud, this book will serve as an introduction to talmudic thought. For the second, readers who are already familiar with talmudic methodology, it will serve as a quick overview of the tractate *Berachot*.

This volume is not intended to be a compilation of conventional insights into the text. *Berachot*, literally, "blessings," deals with our prayers: the *Shema*, the *Amidah*, the blessings said over food and on various occasions. I have selected representative excerpts from this tractate to illustrate each chapter's core ideas. Please note that the commentary accompanying the text may not reflect the conventional interpretation of the *sugya*: It may be my interpretation, or personal understanding, of the passage.

Traditionally, Jews have studied the Talmud in pairs or small groups. I would suggest that you do likewise. Read each *sugya*, each bit of Talmud, out loud, read the commentary either silently or out loud, and then discuss the *sugya* for yourselves, covering the following questions:

What are the rabbis saying?

Why do you think the rabbis included this particular piece of Talmud here?

Do you agree or disagree with the opinion stated?

How do you feel about what you have read?

Will you put this piece of Talmud into practice in your own life? If so, how and why? If not, why not?

In the process of discussing these questions you may find that you are creating your own, new Talmud. That is the ultimate goal of such study: to renew an ancient text by taking it into yourself and adding a bit of yourself to it.

Talmud study is most satisfying when it is more than an intellectual exercise. The more you let the text into your life and soul, the more rewarding Talmud study will be. For example, experience in Jewish living will enrich your Talmud study. The rabbis assumed the people reading their material were already practicing what we would currently call traditional Judaism. They were not providing a manual of basic Jewish law, but rather a guide to the fine points of practice and the reasons behind the rituals. The rabbis assumed that their readers would know that we say the *Shema* every morning and night, that we recite *Birkat HaMazon* after every meal. Therefore, I would suggest that if you are not familiar with traditional Jewish practice, you experience it. Most traditional rabbis will welcome you at their services and are usually able to arrange for you to spend Shabbat with a family that observes the day. If you would rather read about traditional Judaism, I recommend Lis Harris's marvelous book *Holy Days*.

If it sounds as though I'm suggesting that you venture on to a spiritual journey... you're right. Talmud study, the way I'm proposing to do it, touches your soul as well as your mind. It makes you look at someone else's definition of the holy and profane, piety and apostasy, authority and creativity. And if you do it right, it makes you define those things for yourself.

Acknowledgment

I am deeply grateful to have had the opportunity to study this tractate and write about it. I owe a debt of gratitude not only to God, but to many people who have been unfailingly generous with their time and energy. I mention especially:

Arthur Kurzweil and the staff of Jason Aronson, Inc. for giving me this opportunity, and Gloria Jordan, the production editor for this volume, and Nancy Andreola, the copy editor. My thanks also go to:

Rabbi Joseph Radinsky of United Orthodox Synagogues of Houston, Texas, for teaching me Talmud and for reading the manuscript for this book.

Dr. David Kraemer of the Jewish Theological Seminary, for reading the manuscript and sharing his insights with me.

The other persons who read this manuscript and helped shape it: Myra Lipper, Shirley and Bernie Abrams, Deborah Zabarenko, Thea Cooper, Larry Washington, Beth Schwartz, David and Jill Gilbert, and Patrick Doyle.

My Talmud class of Fall 1989 at the Rockville, Maryland, Jewish Community Center and to my confirmation class at Congregation Ner Shalom, Robert Barclay, Michelle Hummel, Lisa Leon, Joe Mintzer, Larry Newdorf, Matthew Rich, and Susie Tendler, all of whom inspired me with their insights into the text. To them goes the credit for the New Year's Eve analogy in Chapter 4, as well as for many other explanations of the text.

Congregation Ner Shalom, Renee Braider, Lucy Zabarenko, and Sonia Zabarenko, for supporting the writing of this work.

Jean Saletan, whose thirst to discover the Talmud's appeal was a source of motivation. I hope this book satisfies her appetite.

Rabbi Jason Z. Edelstein, for his spiritual guidance.

Finally, my loving husband Steven, for his support.

Introduction:
—— What is the Talmud? ——

The Talmud is called the Oral Torah. Tradition has it that God whispered the laws and customs contained in this Torah to Moses on Mount Sinai at the same time God gave Moses the Written Torah (the first five books of the Bible). According to *Pirkei Avot* 1:1, this Oral Torah was passed down through the generations, "from Moses to Joshua; Joshua to the elders; the elders to the prophets; and the prophets handed it down to the men of the Great Assembly."

These "men of the Great Assembly," who governed from approximately 500 to 200 B.C.E., were followed by *zugot*, pairs of leaders. Each *zug*, each pair, was composed of a *Nasi*, the president, and an *Av Beit Din*, the vice-president. The *zugot* presided over the Sanhedrin, the Jewish judicial and legislative body of the era. As in any political body, various factions fought for power. The main combatants of this era were the Sadducees and the Pharisees. The Sadducees believed only in the Written Torah, not in the Oral one, while the Pharisees believed in both. The Sadducees tended to be of a wealthier economic class than the Pharisees. As is often the case, the wealthy were also politically conservative. In addition, they seem to have been more closely linked to the priests, an aristocratic class that ran the Temple cult in Jerusalem, than were the Pharisees. The Sadducees seem to fade from history after the destruction of the Temple by the Romans in 70 C.E. The last of the *zugot* were two teachers named Hillel and Shammai, around whom schools of thought formed.

These two schools existed from the end of the first century B.C.E. until the beginning of the second century C.E. Louis Ginzberg (1955) presents a compelling portrait of these schools in *On Jewish Law and Lore*. He bases his characterization of the two schools on their differing economic interests. He suggests that there were two camps within the Pharisees: conservatives, who assumed that the ancient laws were better and who represented the upper classes (*Beit Shammai*); and liberals, who assumed that the ancient laws might need changing and who represented the poorer classes (*Beit Hillel*). A similar division can be seen in American politics today between conservatives and liberals within *one* political party. For example, among people who call themselves Democrats, there may be liberals and conservatives. The members of *Beit Shammai* and *Beit Hillel* were all Pharisees, yet they had very different approaches to the law and to life.

After the destruction of the Temple in 70 C.E. and the dispersion of the Jews from the Land of Israel, the Pharisees (now called *Tannaim*), who led the Jewish people, had to devise a form of Judaism that could survive this tragedy. The Temple and its sacrifices, which had been the core of Jewish worship, were destroyed. The Sanhedrin, as it functioned in Temple times, was gone. There was no central authority to unify Jewish practice throughout its wide dispersion. Various teachers in various cities taught their own individual traditions. Judaism threatened to disintegrate into small sects whose practices bore little relationship to one another. Something had to be done.

One of the greatest Jewish teachers, Rabbi Akiba, took the situation in hand and began to organize the teachings of individual rabbis into six categories. These became the Six Orders of the Mishnah. Rabbi Judah HaNasi completed this work by compiling an authoritative body of Jewish teaching, which is known as the Mishnah. When Rabbi Judah HaNasi felt that a certain tradition accurately reflected normative Jewish practice and thought, he included it in the Mishnah anonymously, without saying which rabbi taught the tradition. When an opinion was important or interesting but was not the opinion of the majority of rabbis, he attributed it to the rabbi who taught it. To understand the attributions seen so frequently in the Talmud, just imagine the difference it makes when a spokesperson says, "I am speaking in the name of the president (or the Soviet premier or the Queen of England)." Knowing something about the person who makes a statement helps us evaluate that statement's content. In general, an anonymous opinion is adopted as the law over one that is attributed to an individual rabbi. In addition, generally, those opinions stated last in a Mishnah become law.

Rabbi Judah HaNasi, often called simply "Rabbi," completed this work around 200 C.E. Those traditions that he included in his work became known as *mishnayot*. Those that he did not include became known as *baraitot* and *toseftot*. Often, these *baraitot* and *toseftot*—second-string *mishnayot*, if you will— are cited by the *Amoraim*, the rabbis who wrote the Gemara, the commentary on the Mishnah. The Mishnah and Gemara together form the Talmud.

The men who participated in these discussions have different titles. The teachers whose work is preserved in the Mishnah are called *Tannaim*. Many of them had the title rabbi, which means "my teacher." Rabbis received their titles through ordination in the Land of Israel. Descendants of Hillel served as the *Nasi* by hereditary right, and their title was Rabban. The sages of the period after the completion of the Mishnah in 200 C.E. were known as *Amoraim*. The scholars of the Babylonian Talmud were not ordained rabbis, and they gave themselves such titles as *Rav* (master) or *Mar* (mister)—more lowly than the titles Rabbi and Rabban bestowed on the teachers in Palestine. However, their lowly titles belied their power to definitively interpret both the Torah and the Mishnah (see Rivkin 1971, p. 89). All of the *Tannaim* lived in Palestine. Some of the *Amoraim* lived there too, while other *Amoraim* resided in Babylonia. The sages of the era after the Talmud was completed (500 or 600 C.E. in Babylonia) are called *Saboraim*, or *Stamaim*. It is their finished product that we have in our hands today. In this volume, the authorities of both the Mishnah and the Gemara will be referred to as "the rabbis."

Gemara was written in two places: the Land of Israel and Babylonia. The one written in the Land of Israel is called the Palestinian Talmud, or the *Yerushalmi*; the other is the Babylonian Talmud, or *Bavli*. Even though the Land of Israel had been the Jewish national homeland and the birthplace of the Mishnah, the Talmud produced there is less well known and less authoritative than the Babylonian Talmud, which ultimately became the Talmud used to guide everyday life.

The relationship of the Mishnah to the Gemara can be likened to a marriage of two very different people. One is an elegant, get-down-to-business type of few words. The other is chatty, tends to digress, and tries to take everyone's opinion into account. The loquacious partner is guided by the more taciturn one, but in a fight, the former usually wins. Both are pragmatic and idealistic, shrewd and tough, yet principled. The businesslike person is the Mishnah. The Gemara is the much wordier, and ultimately the more authoritative, one. That the Gemara could overrule the Mishnah, and even the Torah, may be puzzling to readers who assumed that the Torah is the highest authority in Judaism, but it is the truth. In general, in Judaism, *hilkheta k'vatraei*—the law follows the latest generation of authorities.

The *Tannaim* and *Amoraim* relate to each other as our Supreme Court relates to the founding fathers. American constitutional law is based upon the Constitution—an elegant, relatively simple document that lays out the fundamental structure and values of American government, a document that can be changed only with great difficulty. Constitutional law as interpreted by the Supreme Court, on the other hand, is everchanging, records both the majority and minority opinions, and operationalizes concepts expressed in the Constitution. The Mishnah corresponds to the Constitution itself. The Gemara corresponds to the process of expounding the Constitution. The founding fathers correspond to the *Tannaim*, and the Judges of the Supreme Court correspond to the *Amoraim*. The Judges are *nominally* inferior to the founding fathers, but in reality, their interpretation of the Constitution overrides the framers' vision of it.

And just as the justices refer to cases that were decided years earlier, so do the rabbis of the Mishnah and Gemara respond to opinions held by rabbis who lived many years before them. The text of the Talmud is like an archaeological dig; it contains strata from various eras of Jewish history. It may seem as if the rabbis are all sitting in a room debating with one another when, in fact, one rabbi may be commenting on something said by another rabbi who lived 200 years before.

Just as constitutional law is formulated in response to society's needs and values, so were the policies found in the Talmud developed according to the requirements and priorities of Jewish society. The *Tannaim* and *Amoraim* formulated Jewish practice in response to the political, economic, and religious pressures the Jewish people faced. For example, Jewish practice was formulated to help Jews withstand the allure of the *minim*. *Minim* seems to be a catchword for several different religious groups who challenged Judaism's validity: Christians, Gnostics (those who believed in two gods, a good one and an evil one), and pagans. The rabbis were trying to convince their readers that their system of religious thought was the truest *and* facilitate their readers' use of that system.

The rabbis' works are organized in a way that outlines their basic message quite clearly. For example, the tractate we will study, *Berachot*, serves as a guide to Jewish prayer. This topic was of crucial importance to the rabbis. The Jews' relationship with God had been shaken by the Temple's destruction. Finding a uniform way that Jews could rebuild that relationship, as a community and as individuals, was of primary importance to the rabbis. Therefore, they composed this tractate: a step-by-step outline for building a complete, intense, and satisfying relationship with God.

The contents of this tractate follow a specific, logical order that reveals much about what the rabbis believed was most important in building a relationship with God. As we move through the tractate, we begin with the most basic subjects and progress to more unusual ones. We also move from those ways of relating to God that allow for the least individuality (that is, saying the *Shema*) to those allowing the most individuality (that is, prayers said over personal experiences). We also move through the chronology of a day as we move through the tractate: we begin with the evening *Shema* (Jewish days begin at night), then proceed to the morning *Shema*, then to the *Tefillah* (which is said after the *Shema*), then to blessings related to eating (which are said after prayer), and finally, to prayers for events that might happen during the course of a day, such as the acquisition of a new piece of property.

Interestingly, the issue of whether laws are derived from the Torah *(De'Oraita)* or are edicts of the rabbis *(De'Rabbanan)* does not appear to be a principle used to organize the material of this tractate. This is logical. The rabbis wanted their dictates to carry as much, or more, weight as any others mentioned earlier in the chain of tradition. Often, in fact, the rabbis will use their power to define biblical laws out of practical existence. For example, the Torah commands parents to kill a son who acts stubbornly and rebelliously toward them (Deuteronomy 21:18-21) but the rabbis restrict the definitions of *son* and *parents* so severely that it makes it impossible for this law to be applied (*Sanhedrin* 45b). The rabbis can actually overrule the Torah by making theirs the accepted interpretation of it. Thus, they would have been unlikely to emphasize the different origins of the laws. In essence, they want all laws to be interpreted as *De'Rabbanan*—that is, according to their definitions.

Discussions in this tractate often operate on at least two levels. On the one hand, the rabbis are discussing some practical question that must be decided. On the other hand, they are also addressing an underlying philosophical issue. Often, when the rabbis seem to be getting off track, they are simply moving from the first level to the second. So, for example, on one level the rabbis may be discussing the question of what to do with your *tefillin* when you enter a privy. But on another level, they are trying to determine how to deal with the meeting of the holy (the words of the Torah inside the *tefillin*) and the profane (the privy) in general. Understanding the broad issues that underlie each specific case makes even a discussion about a privy interesting and meaningful.

The tractate is also organized according to the principles used to compose our prayer book, specifically:

1. *Tadir* and *sh'eino tadir*: **That which happens most regularly precedes that which happens less regularly.** We begin with the *Shema* and *Amidah*, which are said at least twice every day, and move to prayers over food (which might not be said twice every day),

and so forth. In practical terms, this principle can be illustrated by the following example: if you have the opportunity to greet both your spouse and the president of the United States, this rule would have you greet your spouse first, then the president, presuming that you greet your spouse more regularly than you greet the president. In Hebrew, that which happens most regularly is called *tadir*. That which happens less regularly is called *sh'eino tadir*.

2. **When there are several texts regarding the same issue, include all of them.** We see this in the prayer book several times. For example, the prayer immediately before the *Shema* always describes God's great love for us. However, the texts of this prayer are different in the morning and evening services. Why? Because the sages who composed the prayer book had two versions of the prayer at hand and, in this way, included both.

3. **Conclusions of sections, chapters, and the whole tractate are marked by *nechemtot* (*nechemtah*, singular, a message of comfort and/or redemption).** Many of our prayers end with a wish for peace, as does this tractate (see Chapter 9).

This tractate of the Talmud teaches us the steps, and the skills, that will bring us to a full relationship with God. It has two main sections: Chapters 1 through 5 and Chapters 6 through 9. In Chapter 1, the sages define this basic relationship: *an intense, monogamous relationship of one soul and the one God which encompasses all our experiences, good and bad, and is expressed in time through* mitzvot *and Torah study*. In Chapter 2, they teach us how to deal with interferences in that relationship. Chapter 3 shows us how to relate to God when our experiences do not just interfere, but might even destroy, our ability to reach out to God—when a family member dies, for example, or when we feel impure. These three chapters outline our most basic relationship with God.

The next two chapters deal with what the rabbis consider the next most important prayer after the *Shema*, the *Tefillah*, also called the *Shemoneh Esrei* or *Amidah*. This prayer allows us to express more individuality than does the *Shema*. In the *Shema* we express our love of God. In the *Tefillah*, we express our love of God, *and* ask God for blessings we need, such as sustenance and health. In Chapter 4, we learn about this basic interaction of prayer and personality. Chapter 5 covers more extreme cases of the same phenomenon: extreme devotion to God (piety) and a complete breakdown in the relationship (apostasy). These first five chapters form a unit: they all deal with our direct communication with God in a prayerful setting.

The last four chapters address our communication with God away from set moments of prayer. In Chapter 6, we learn how to direct our appetites for pleasure toward God—making our desires holy instead of profane. In Chapter 7, we learn who belongs in a group that prays outside the synagogue and what criteria are used to determine who may form such a group. Chapter 8 extends the theme of Chapter 7 and shows us not only who *belongs*, but who has *authority* in our larger group, the Jewish people. This chapter also explores the ways in which we can use our intellect as a means to reach out to God. Finally, Chapter 9 covers some of the most out-of-the-ordinary ways we encounter God: in thunder, lightning, rainbows, dreams, and the like. The experiences outlined in this last chapter constitute the least predictable, and often most amazing, moments of contact with the Divine. The Talmud gives us the means to frame these experiences in terms of our overarching relationship with God. The organization of the chapters in this tractate can be summarized as follows:

1. Relating to God in exclusively prayerful ways
   Basic relationship with God: Chapters 1, 2, and 3
   Expressing our needs to God: Chapters 4 and 5
2. Relating to God outside of specified, regular moments of prayer
   Consecrating our desires: Chapter 6
   Worshipping God in a group: Chapters 7 and 8
   Meeting God in moments of wonder: Chapter 9

The Talmud became the basis of Jewish practice and thought. It guides every aspect of traditional Jewish life, from the way one dresses to what one eats. On the other hand, liberal Jews do not believe that the Mishnah and Gemara were given to Moses on Mount Sinai. (For that matter, many liberal Jews do not believe that the Torah was given there, either.) Rather, they believe that these are holy and wonderful works, inspired by God, but written by people. Therefore, Reform Jews do not believe that the Talmud has a binding authority. Conservative and Reconstructionist Jews believe that the Talmud has some degree of authority but that it can be differed with, following certain guidelines.

The Talmud has been printed in the same format for several hundred years; each page has been arranged the same way, regardless of who published it. In the center is the text of the Mishnah, followed by the commentary of the Gemara. This central text is surrounded by the commentaries of the great eleventh-century rabbi Rashi, later commentators, called Tosaphists, and others. (In Europe during the last century, some scholars knew the Talmud so well that they could stick a pin anywhere on a page of the Talmud and then recite every word that the pin passed through on every page in the whole tractate!) These pages are numbered as "folios"; that is, the front of the page is, let us say, 11a, and the back is 11b. When quoting from the Talmud, we still cite the page number and the side of the page from which the passage comes.

The translations of the Talmud used in this book are adapted from the Soncino edition by Maurice Simon, first published in 1948. Although I have used gender-inclusive language in my commentary, I have used translations that reflect the fact that the male gender predominates in language used to describe God in the Talmud.

1

What Is Our Basic Relationship with God?

Many a love story begins with a wedding scene. Two parties stand together and express their devotion and commitment to each other. This tractate begins and, as we will see, ends with just such a statement of love and commitment. In Judaism, that statement of commitment between God and Israel is made, not with an exchange of vows, but through the recital of the *Shema*. For the rabbis, the *Shema* expresses the terms of our relationship with God. They defined that relationship as *an intense, monogamous relationship of one soul and the one God which encompasses all our experiences, good and bad, and is expressed in time through* mitzvot *and Torah study*. We will explore this definition concept by concept in this chapter. Our first text introduces many of these themes.

MISHNAH (2a): From what time may one recite the *Shema* in the evening? From the time that the priests enter [their houses] in order to eat their *terumah* until the end of the first watch. These are the word of Rabbi Eliezer. And the sages say: until midnight. Rabban Gamaliel says: until the dawn comes up.

It is told that once his sons were coming home [late] from a feast. They said to him: "We have not yet recited the [evening] *Shema*." He said to them, "If the dawn has not yet come up you are obligated to recite it." And not in respect to this alone did they so decide, but wherever the sages said "until midnight," the obligation to perform the mitzvah extends until the dawn

3

comes up . . . . If this is so, then why did the sages say "until midnight"? To keep a man far from transgression.

This mishnah is complicated because, as the first one in the tractate, many of the most important dimensions that will be used to analyze questions throughout this entire volume are introduced in it. Think of it as the beginning of a play, where each of the leading characters is quickly presented to the audience. The players are as follows:

1. **Judaism is a religion of relationships in time.** Maintaining relationships is of prime importance in Judaism, including the maintenance of our relationship with God. One of the ways we stay in touch with God is through the daily recital of the *Shema*; this prayer is a day-by-day reaffirmation of the terms of our relationship. This affirmation used to happen in the Temple in Jerusalem, through the sacrifices and the recital of the *Shema*. After the destruction of the Temple, however, the Jewish people no longer had the sacrifices to help them express and maintain their relationship with God. Therefore, Judaism began to construct a space in which to relate with God out of time. Time became the medium in which we create holiness. We set aside certain times for prayer, for rest, for holidays. The first dimension, the first *word* of the whole tractate, is *when*, emphasizing that time is the key to maintaining the relationship.

The system of counting time in the ancient world was quite different from ours. Each day and night was divided into 12 "hours," no matter what the season. Therefore, the length of an hour depended on the season of the year. There were three "watches" each day and each night—hence, six altogether.

This mishnah defines "night" in terms of the *Shema*. Just as we often define distance in terms of time ("How far away is it?" "About 20 minutes from here"), the rabbis define time in terms of our relationship with God.

This mishnah begins with the first recitation of the *Shema* in a day, since Jewish days begin in the evening. Why? Because, in Genesis, after the first day of creation, the Torah says, "and there was *evening* and there was morning, one day" (Genesis 1:5), with the evening mentioned before the morning. If it had said, "and there was *morning* and there was evening," our days would begin in the morning.

2. *Tumah* (ritual impurity), *Taharah* (ritual purity) and the Temple cult. If the priests who performed the sacrifices in the Temple were ritually unclean *(tamei)*, they were not permitted to eat the *terumah* until they had taken a ritual bath and the sun had set. *Terumah* literally means "that which is lifted or separated" and was an offering to be given to the priest. There were two types of *terumah*: the regular offering, which the Israelites had to separate from their own crops and give to the priest, and the *terumat ma'aser*, the tithe offering, which the Levites had to separate for the priests from the tithes they received. For a very detailed and graphic description of the Temple cult that helps make its appeal clear, read Emil Schurer's description in *The History of the Jewish People in the Age of Jesus Christ (75 B.C.–135 A.D.)*. By the time the Talmud was completed, ritual purity was not as crucial a category as it had been when the Temple stood. The categories *kodesh* (holy) and *chol* (profane) became more important. These categories will be examined in detail in Chapter 3.

3. *Din* and *lifnim mishurat haDin*. The tension between the minimum the law requires and the norm the culture desires. *Din*, the law, by its very nature can legislate only the minimum behavior required for the basic functioning of society. Therefore, the law in this case is the minimum: the evening *Shema* may be said until dawn. However, this is not the most desirable way to say the evening *Shema*. Therefore, the rabbis make "a fence around the Torah" (*Pirkei Avot* 1:1) and encourage a standard of behavior that is beyond the letter of the law. The rabbis wanted to build safeguards into the system of Jewish observance. Therefore, if the deadline for saying the evening *Shema* is actually dawn, they ruled that it may be said until midnight in order to keep people from pressing the limit and risk transgressing this commandment.

4. *DeOraita/ DeRabbanan.* The (apparent) primacy of commands that are derived directly from the Torah over the dictates of the rabbis. (In point of fact, dictates of the rabbis were often upheld more strictly than laws derived directly from

the Torah.) The rabbis believed that the obligation to read the *Shema* comes from the Torah itself. The *V'ahavta* states, "You shall speak of them . . . when you lie down and when you rise up" (Deuteronomy 6:7). The rabbis interpret this to mean that we are commanded to say the *Shema*, *as they define it*, in the morning and evening.

The rabbis define the *Shema* as three paragraphs: Deuteronomy 6:4–9; Deuteronomy 11:13–21; and Numbers 15:37–41. (In Reform prayer books, it is Deuteronomy 6:4–9 and Numbers 15:40–41.) These three paragraphs are surrounded by blessings praising God for creating the world, for giving us the Torah, and for redeeming us from Egypt. In the evening an additional prayer is added, asking God to protect our souls overnight.

5. **The role of personalities in shaping the tradition.** The personalities of individual teachers shaped their opinions. It is therefore important to know whether a view is voiced by the majority—often indicated here by the phrase "the sages said"—or by one rabbi. If an individual states an opinion, it is important to know as much about this person as possible, since this background data will help us evaluate the opinion.

In this mishnah, two early *Tannaim* voice characteristic views. Rabbi Eliezer (ben Hyrkanos), a second-generation (80–120) *Tanna*, was a faithful conservator of decisions handed down from earlier generations and opposed even the slightest modification in them. In general, he seems to have had a strict, even harsh, personality. When his brother-in-law, Rabban Gamaliel, excommunicated him, Rabbi Eliezer became so upset that he prayed for Gamaliel to die (*Baba Metsia* 59b), and his prayer was apparently efficacious. (See Chapter 8 for more on this story.)

Rabban Gamaliel was also a second-generation *Tanna*. After the Second Temple was destroyed in 70 C.E. and Jerusalem came under Roman occupation, the spiritual center for Judaism moved to the academy founded by Rabbi Johanan ben Zakkai in Yavneh, a town in Judea. Rabban Gamaliel succeeded Rabbi Johanan ben Zakkai and became the president of this academy. He wanted to secure Yavneh's status as the spiritual center of

Judaism, and to that end he exercised his authority as *Nasi* (president of the Academy) so harshly that he was eventually expelled from office (see Chapter 4). He was, however, reinstated shortly thereafter.

You can begin to see why it is so important to know who is stating which opinion. Knowing where they are coming from, both personally and philosophically, helps us weigh their statements more judiciously. In this mishnah, Rabbi Eliezer simply quotes an older practice, dating from the time when the Temple still stood. He does not suggest a new way to determine when to say the *Shema* now that the Temple is gone. However, it is his opinion, in a redefined form, that becomes the law. We may say the *Shema* from the time when the priests would have gone out to eat their *terumah*—that is, when three small stars are visible in the sky. The views of both Rabban Gamaliel and the sages are adopted. The *Shema may* be said until dawn, but is *best* said before midnight to ensure that it will be recited at the proper time.

The five dimensions introduced in this first mishnah will be used throughout this tractate to shed light on a wide variety of questions.

Our next *sugya* illustrates how much time and our relationship with God define each other in Judaism.

> **GEMARA (3a):** Rav Isaac bar Samuel said in the name of Rav: "The night has three watches, and at each watch the Holy One, blessed be He, sits and roars like a lion and says, 'Woe to the children, that because of their sins I destroyed My house and burnt My Temple and exiled them among the nations of the world.'"
>
> It has been taught: Rabbi Jose said, "One time I was walking on the road, and I entered a certain ruin among the ruins of Jerusalem to pray. Elijah, may his memory be for good, came and waited for me at the door till I finished my prayer. After I finished my prayer, he said to me, 'Peace be with you, my rabbi!'
>
> And I replied, 'Peace be with you my rabbi and my teacher!'
>
> And he said to me, 'My son, why did you go into this ruin?'
>
> I replied, 'To pray.'
>
> And he said to me, 'You ought to have prayed on the road.'

And I said to him, 'I feared lest passers-by might interrupt me.'

And he said to me, 'You ought to have said an abbreviated prayer.'

In that one moment, I learned from him three things: I learned that one does not enter a ruin. And I learned that one may pray on the road. And I learned that one who prays on the road prays a short prayer.

And he said (further) to me, 'My son, what sound did you hear in this ruin?'

And I said to him, 'I heard a *Bat Kol* [a Divine voice], cooing like a dove, and saying, "Woe to the children, that because of their sins I destroyed My house and burnt My Temple and exiled them among the nations of the world."

And he said to me, 'By your life and by the life of your head [an exclamation], not in this moment alone does it so exclaim, but thrice each day does it exclaim thus!'

'And not only that, whenever the Jewish people enter their synagogues and houses of study and respond [during the Kaddish], "May His great name be blessed," the Holy One, blessed be He, shakes His head and says, "Happy is the king who is thus praised in his house! Woe to the father who had to banish his children, and woe to the children who had to be banished from the table of their father!"'"

Like our first mishnah, this *sugya* has many levels. First of all, it relates time to God. Time is not a physical phenomenon in Judaism; it is a religious one. God keeps time with Israel. As each watch in the night passes, God thinks about the Jewish people. And what does God think? In one version of the story God blames the people of Israel for their misdeeds, for which they have been severely punished: their Temple was destroyed and they were exiled from the Land of Israel. *Minim* (see the Introduction) often taunted the Jews on account of this punishment. The *minim* believed that this exile and God's failure to rebuild the Temple were proof that the God of Judaism did not exist, had no power, or had forsaken the Jews.

For obvious reasons, these assertions troubled the rabbis, so they developed ways to help themselves maintain their faith while coping with their "punishment" of exile. To assert that God sits in Heaven and laments Israel's sinfulness three times a night was not helpful in this task, even if it explained why the Jews were in their current predicament. Such a story provides no hope of redemption to its Jewish listeners.

That is why they immediately soften Rav Isaac's version of Rav's story. The second story (Rabbi Jose's) expresses a much more balanced view of Israel's relationship with God and provides more hope to its listeners. Note how, even though Rav lived after Rabbi Jose, the redactors of the Talmud put Rabbi Jose's version last, and thus let it "overrule" Rav's harsher vision of God. (If they had wanted Rav's version to prevail, they could have put it at the end of Rabbi Jose's and framed it as the most salient quote from the whole story.)

In Rabbi Jose's version, God still laments Israel's sins, but the lament is heard in the cooing of a dove rather than the roaring of a lion. God grieves three times each day and each night, according to the "watches," over which we have no control. But we can control our own behavior. We control when we go to the synagogue and the house of study, and we can thus control how God feels about us. Hearing our praises, God is pleased and expresses not just a lament at Israel's sins, but love as well. And we can please God in this way more often than six times in 24 hours. In other words, it is our actions that swing the balance such that God rejoices more than God laments. The rabbis see our relationship with God as a close one. We affect God's feelings and we are constantly in God's thoughts.

This second version appeals to the rabbis much more than the first. God expresses not only judgment of the Jews, but love for them. We are not left with a feeling of powerlessness and hopelessness: God has judged us and there is nothing we can do to make things better. Rather, we are given the means— prayer and study—to find our way back to God.

It is interesting that Rabbi Jose, who lived closer to the time of the Temple's destruction, gives a more gentle version of God's lament than does Rav, who lived later. This may simply reflect Rabbi Jose's kind nature, but it may also reflect the growing despair that the Jewish people felt as time went on and the Temple was not rebuilt.

We should add a word about Elijah in the Talmud. He is sort of a magic figure—turning up when needed, providing advice on how to develop Jewish law, acting as God's messenger. In this *sugya*, he sounds like a concerned parent. He does not want Rabbi Jose to endanger himself by praying in a ruin, where debris could fall on him, where robbers could attack him, or where demons were thought to dwell. This pragmatic view of prayer is found throughout this tractate: pray, but do not endanger yourself on its account.

One of the hallmarks of our basic relationship with God is that it encompasses all the experiences of our lives, the good and the bad. The rabbis attempt to explain how suffering fit into that relationship in this next *sugya*.

> **GEMARA (5a)**: Rabba, and some say Rav Chisda, said, "If a man sees that sufferings come to him, let him examine his conduct. For it is said, 'Let us search and try our ways, and return unto the Lord' (Lamentations 3:40). If he examined [his deeds] and did not find [anything objectionable], let him attribute it to the neglect of the study of the Torah. For it is said, 'Happy is the man whom God chastens, and is taught from Your Torah' (Psalms 94:12). If he did attribute it [thus], and [still] did not find [this to be the cause], then it is known that these are chastenings of love, for it is said, 'For those God loves, He reproves' (Proverbs 3:12)."

For any religion to be effective, it must explain the existence of suffering and evil. Rabba's explanation is representative of Jewish thought on this subject. It focuses on each person's responsibility for his or her fate. If something bad has happened to you, first examine your own conduct to see whether you are being punished. Note that we are to look at our *conduct*, not our *selves*. We may choose to behave sinfully or righteously. Regardless of our choices, however, the rabbis assume that each of us has within our basic nature some innate goodness.

The rabbis believed that God rewards and punishes us for our deeds, either here on earth or after we die, in the World to Come. They held that God (1) controls history, rewarding and punishing individuals and nations and (2) is completely just. Therefore, when a righteous, studious person was suffering what appeared to be an undeserved punishment, the rabbis had to find some explanation that would reconcile this seemingly arbitrary punishment with their vision of God. This reconciliation is found in the concept *yisurim shel ahava*, chastenings of love. These are trials that God lays on the righteous in this world in order to reward them for their heroic faith in the World to Come. Of course, this concept comforts only those who truly believe in an afterlife in which they will be rewarded.

The rabbis make it clear that suffering is a part of our relationship with God. We do not have to like it, and we are allowed to resist it, but we must grapple with it. (On page 5b of this tractate, three stories are told of rabbis who fell ill and stated that neither their suffering nor its rewards was welcome to them.)

Part of every relationship is communication. In our basic relationship, one of the ways we relate to God is through the *mitzvot*. This is one of the ways in which God relates to us, as well: the *mitzvot* are mutually binding.

> **GEMARA (6a)**: Rav Nachman bar Isaac said to Rav Hiyya bar Avin, "What is written in the *tefillin* of the Lord of the Universe? He replied to him: 'And who is like Your people Israel, a nation unique in the earth?' (I Chronicles 17:21). Does then, the Holy One, blessed be He, sing the praises of Israel? Yes. For it is written, 'You have avouched the Lord this day... and the Lord has avouched you this day' (Deuteronomy 26:17, 18).
>
> The Holy One, blessed be He, said to Israel, 'You have made me a single entity in the world, and I shall make you a single entity in the world.' 'You have made me a single entity in the world,' as it is said, 'Hear O Israel, the Lord our God, the Lord is one' (Deuteronomy 6:4).' 'And I shall make you a single entity in the world,' as it is said, 'And who is like Your people Israel, a nation unique in the earth?'" (I Chronicles 17:21).

Just as wedding rings symbolize a couple's bond to each other, so the *tefillin* symbolize the commitment God and the Jewish people have made to each other. The *tefillin* are the physical presence of the *Shema* in our lives. The *tefillin* contain four paragraphs from the Torah: Exodus 13:1–10, Exodus 13:11–16, Deuteronomy 6:4–9, and Deuteronomy 11:13–21. Each of these sections contains an almost identical passage requiring us to put "these words" as "a sign upon your hand and as frontlets between your eyes." In addition, both of the passages from Deuteronomy state "and you shall bind them." The rabbis interpreted these words as a commandment to perform a specific, concrete act. They devised the *tefillin*, small black boxes containing "these words," bound to the hand and head, to fulfill that commandment. Since the Torah designates that they should be a sign (singular) on the hand, they connect the four parchments in the *tefillah* of the hand, making it a single scroll. And since they are to be frontlets (plural) between our eyes, there are four separate parchments in the *tefillah* of the head.

The fact that the rabbis envisioned God wearing *tefillin* tells us a great deal about how they viewed our basic relationship with God. They believed God was bound by the Torah just as we are. The commandments are not a one-way street. They are an expression of mutual love, responsibility, and commitment between the people of Israel and God and, as such, are shared by both parties. In many ways, the Torah is like a *ketubah*, a wedding contract between God and the Jewish people.

This reciprocity is reflected in the contents of God's *tefillin*. God does not merely don *tefillin* as a mechanical act of solidarity with Israel. God wears *tefillin* that express God's love for us as a unique people, just as our *tefillin* express our love for God, and our recognition of God's uniqueness.

This reciprocity is an integral part of the relationship.

> **GEMARA (6b):** Ravin bar Rav Adda said in the name of Rabbi Isaac, "Everyone who goes regularly to the synagogue, and then does not come one day, the Holy One, blessed be He, makes inquiry about him."

This short *sugya* is endearing and telling. Our relationship with God is based on mutual dependence. *God counts on us* to be at services, just as we count on God to be available when we pray. Prayer is our time set aside for communication with God, and if we miss it, even for just one day, God misses us.

This vision of God may not fit our modern ideas about the Deity. There is a tendency to view God as needing nothing from us, to believe that we may make our supplications to God without giving God anything in return. This is not the Jewish view of our basic relationship with God. Rather, Judaism sees the relationship as a reciprocal one.

A distinguishing feature of our reciprocal relationship with God is *kavanah*—intensity, or intention.

> **GEMARA (6b)**: Rabbi Zera says, "The merit of attending a lecture lies in the running [to it] . . ."
>
> Rava says, "The merit of hearing a law lies in the understanding of the reasoning behind it."
>
> Rav Pappa says, "The merit of attending a house of mourning lies in the silence observed."
>
> Mar Zutra says, "The merit of a fast day lies in the charity dispensed."
>
> Rav Shesheth says, "The merit of a eulogy lies in the raising the voice [in crying it brings forth]."
>
> Rav Ashi says, "The merit of attending a wedding lies in the words [of congratulation addressed to the bride and bridegroom]."

Each of the foregoing examples shows it is possible to be with people who are experiencing something important and intense and yet disengage ourselves from the significance and emotion of the moment. The rabbis emphasized that this is not acceptable. It is not enough to visit a house of mourning and then make idle chitchat. We must feel the mourners' pain, keep silent, and allow them to grieve. Going through the motions is not enough. Similarly, we must be eager to internalize what we learn and make it part of ourselves. We must be present and engaged with all our hearts.

This is especially true, of course, when we say the *Shema*. The *Shema* is the only prayer in the service that *must* be said with *kavanah*—true intention. That is why we close our eyes when we say the *Shema*—so that we can concentrate on it completely. The ability to make connections with others, and feel empathy for them, is a hallmark of our relationship with God. God feels our pains and joys, and we can hope to be able to feel some of God's sorrow and rejoicing.

The rabbis continue to define our relationship with God by identifying that part of a human being that is most like God: the soul.

> **GEMARA (10a)**: He said to him [Rabbi Shimi to Rabbi Simeon ben Pazzi], "What I meant to tell you is this. To whom did David refer in these five verses beginning with 'Bless the Lord, O my soul?'"
>
> 1. "Bless the Lord, O my soul; and all that is within me, bless His holy name." (Psalms 103:1)
> 2. "Bless the Lord, O my soul, and forget not all His benefits." (Psalms 103:2)
> 3. "Bless the Lord, all ye His works, in all places of His dominion; Bless the Lord, O my soul." (Psalms 103:22)
> 4. "Bless the Lord, O my soul. O Lord, my God, Thou art very great." (Psalms 104:1)
> 5. "Let sinners cease out of the earth and let the wicked be no more. Bless the Lord, O my soul. Hallelujah." (Psalms 104:35)
>
> "He was alluding only to the Holy One, blessed be He, and to the soul.
>
> Just as the Holy One, blessed be He, fills the whole world, so the soul fills the body.
>
> Just as the Holy One, blessed be He, sees, but is not seen, so the soul sees, but is not itself seen.
>
> Just as the Holy One, blessed be He, feeds the whole world, so the soul feeds the whole body.
>
> Just as the Holy One, blessed be He, is pure, so the soul is pure.
>
> Just as the Holy One, blessed be He, abides in the innermost precincts [of the Temple], so the soul abides in the innermost precincts.
>
> Let one who has these five qualities in him [that is, one who has a soul], come and praise Him who has these five qualities."

The rabbis define the soul as that part of us that most resembles God. As God fills the world, so our souls fill our bodies. The soul feeds us, is pure and invisible, and dwells deep within us just as God feeds the world, is pure, invisible, and dwells deep within the Temple. The rabbis tie these five qualities to the five times that David, who they believed wrote the psalms, used the phrase "Bless the Lord, O my soul" in those works. These five phrases are also tied to five stages in David's life, ranging from before birth to the moment of death (p.10 a). In other words, the one soul, by its very nature, corresponds to the One God throughout our lives.

For the rabbis, we human beings are little lower than the angels, yet we are far from Divine. God's nature is so lofty, and so different from ours, that we might feel discouraged trying to communicate with God. Therefore, they demonstrate that there is something in us, the soul, that is like God and can relate to God.

We relate to God through the *mitzvot*, through our souls, and through the study of Torah. But Torah study is not necessarily part of the relationship: it must be done with the proper intention. If we study Torah as an intellectual exercise alone, it will not serve this purpose. In the next *sugya*, the rabbis offer prayers to say before Torah study to help us direct our energies toward God during this activity.

GEMARA (11b): What benediction is said [before the study of the Torah]? Rav Judah said in the name of Samuel, "[Blessed are You, O Lord, Ruler of the Universe] who has sanctified us by Your commandments, and commanded us to study the words of Torah."

Rabbi Johanan used to conclude as follows, "Please make pleasant, therefore, we beseech You, O Lord our God, the words of Your Torah in our mouths and in the mouths of Your people, the house of Israel, and let us, and our children, and the children of Your people, the house of Israel, all know Your name and occupy themselves with Your Torah. Blessed are You, O Lord, who teaches Torah to His people Israel."

Rav Hamnuna said, "[Blessed are You, O Lord, Ruler of the Universe] who has chosen us from all the nations and given us His Torah. Blessed are You, O Lord, who gives the Torah."

Rav Hamnuna said, "This is the finest of the benedictions. Therefore let us say all of them."

Each of these blessings is used during Jewish worship services. The last one is the blessing said over the reading of the Torah during services. The first one may be said any time we commence the study of the Written or Oral Torah. This blessing is also said as part of the preliminary prayers preceding the morning service. In the prayer book, it is followed by Rabbi Johanan's blessing, then by passages from the Torah, Mishnah, and Gemara that are to be studied.

This composition reflects two principles of Jewish liturgy. First, we say a blessing and then perform an act immediately afterward, without interruption. Occasionally, we say a blessing immediately *after* we perform an action—for example, when lighting the candles on Shabbat evening.

Making a blessing without performing a *mitzvah* is deemed a *brachah l'vatalah*, a prayer said in vain, and is prohibited. Second, when the redactors of the prayer book had a choice between two or more versions of a blessing, they included as many of them as possible.

Why was Rabbi Hamnuna's blessing considered the best? Perhaps because the first blessing emphasizes God almost exclusively, and the second focuses on us and our offspring. However, the third one (the one chosen), focuses on the relationship created between God and the people of Israel by the Torah. The gift of Torah is an affirmation of God's choosing, and loving, us.

The last mishnah of Chapter 1 is a *nechemtah*, a message of comfort and hope that mentions the Exodus from Egypt, the paradigm of redemption.

> **MISHNAH (12b)**: The Exodus from Egypt is to be mentioned [in the Shema] at night-time. Said Rabbi Eleazer ben Azariah, "Behold, I am like one seventy years old, and I have never been worthy [to find a reason why] the Exodus from Egypt should be mentioned at night-time until Ben Zoma expounded it, for it says, 'That you may remember the day when you came forth out of the land of Egypt all the days of your life' (Deuteronomy 16:3). 'The days of your life' [refers only to] the days. But *all* the days of your life' includes the night [as well]. But the sages say, 'the days of your life' refers to this world: 'all the days of your life' is to add the days of the Messiah."

This mishnah refers to the third paragraph of the *Shema*, which makes mention of the *tallit* and the Exodus. One might think it would be recited only during the day, since that is when we fulfill the *mitzvah* of seeing the *tsitsit*. (The *tsitsit* are not worn at night, because the commandment is to *see* them, not wear them. The rabbis assumed we would not be able to see the *tsitsit* at night.) However, this paragraph is still recited in the evening because it mentions the Exodus from Egypt. This midrash is included in the *Haggadah*, the service for the first night of Passover.

The sages' interpretation of Deuteronomy 16:3 calls to mind the ultimate redemption that will come at the end of time. The rabbis believed that the Torah was perfect and that every word in it held deep meaning.

Therefore, there had to be some significance to the text mentioning "all" the days of our lives. They concluded that it must refer to this life and the life after death. Here, in one concise mishnah, we have many of our most basic themes: our basic relationship with God expressed through the *Shema* and the Torah, as the rabbis interpreted it, and a belief in God's ultimate reward for faithfulness to the relationship in the World to Come.

2

What Interferes with Our Relationship with God?

I magine you are Don Larsen, the pitcher for the New York Yankees in the 1956 World Series. It is the ninth inning, and you have already struck two batters out. If you strike this next batter out, you will win the game and pitch the first-ever perfect game in the World Series. As you peer at Yogi Berra, your catcher, you do not hear the crowd or even the rapid beating of your own heart. You are concentrating intensely. Your entire being is focused on getting that ball into Yogi's mitt.

That ability to direct one's whole being intensely is called, in Hebrew, *kavanah*, or intention. *Kavanah*, intensity, is the hallmark of our basic relationship with God. A prayer must be said with deep concentration to be considered sincere—the same kind of fierce concentration a pitcher trains on his catcher. In the rabbis' view, dealing with outside events or intrinsic conditions which prevent us from having *kavanah*, is the subject of this chapter. As they move through this topic, the rabbis outline such interferences, starting with the most external and easy-to-manage ones, and progressing to more inward and ingrained obstacles to our relationship with God.

MISHNAH (13a): If one was reading in the Torah [the portion of the Shema] when the time for its recital arrived, if he had the intention [to fulfill that *mitzvah* in] his heart, he has performed his obligation.

In the breaks, one may give greeting out of respect and return greeting. In the middle [of a section] one may give greeting out

21

of fear and return it, so [said] Rabbi Meir. Rabbi Judah says: in the middle one may give greeting out of fear and return it out of respect, in the breaks one may give greeting out of respect and return greeting to anyone. The breaks are as follows: between the first blessing and the second, between the second and "Hear (Shema)," between "Hear" and "and it shall come to pass," between "and it shall come to pass" and "and the Lord said" and between "and the Lord said" and "true and firm." Rabbi Judah says, between "and the Lord said" and "true and firm" one should not interrupt.

Rabbi Joshua ben Korchah said, why was the section of "Hear" placed before that of "and it shall come to pass"? So that one should first accept upon himself the yoke of the kingdom of heaven and only then take upon himself the yoke of the commandments. Why does the section of "and it shall come to pass" come before that of "and the Lord said"? Because [the section] "and it shall come to pass" is carried out both day and night, whereas [the section] "and the Lord said" is carried out only in the day.

Our mishnah begins by demonstrating that intention is prayer's distinguishing feature. In the first situation outlined, the *Tannaim* posit that someone studying Torah happens to read the *Shema* and *V'ahavtah* (Deuteronomy 6:4–9) at the time when he is supposed to recite this passage as a prayer. Has he fulfilled his obligation to recite the *Shema* just by reading it? Or is something more required? Something more *is* required—*kavanah*.

No other prayer *must* be said with intention. Ideally, of course, we would say all our prayers in a state of deep devotion. But the rabbis of the Talmud recognized that this is impossible. So they legislated that only the first line of the *Shema* must be said with intention at each utterance.

Having determined that the *Shema* must be said with true intention, the rabbis begin to discuss those events that can interfere with our concentration. They start with the most likely scenario: the need to greet someone during prayer. Imagine you are in synagogue reciting the *Shema*. Your friend, your parent, or your teacher passes by and wants to exchange greetings with you. If you stop in the middle of the *Shema* to exchange greetings, you might feel as if you are interrupting your conversation with God. However, if your friend passes by and you fail to greet him or her, and then you worry about having snubbed your friend, you also may not be able to concentrate. Therefore, the rabbis worked out this intricate system that allows us to balance our needs to relate to God *and* to others.

Whom should we properly fear, and whom should we respect? The definitions of the rabbis are not what we might expect them to be. There is even some disagreement among modern commentators as to the exact meanings of these talmudic categories. Rashi defines someone we should honor as one sufficiently greater than ourselves whom, out of respect, we feel we should approach in greeting rather than expecting him or her to greet us first. He defines someone to fear as an individual who would kill you if you did not greet him. The great modern talmud scholar, Adin Steinsaltz, offers a different definition of this last category. He contends that those you are to fear are the ones the Torah itself tells you to fear (such as your mother and father, as it says in Leviticus 19:3, "Each person should fear his mother and father").

Intuitively, the rabbis understood that greeting people is more of an interruption than responding to greetings, so they developed a more liberal policy regarding responses. The *halachah*, Jewish law, follows both Rabbi Judah and Rabbi Meir. The breaks are between the prayers that surround the *Shema* and between the paragraphs of the *Shema* itself. One should not make a break between the end of the *Shema* and the beginning of the next prayer (*emet v'Emunah* in the evening and *emet v'Yatsiv* in the morning).

The last segment of this mishnah reveals some of the underlying principles used to organize our liturgy. Here the rabbis answer the question "Why are the paragraphs of the *Shema* arranged in the order in which we find them?" They are arranged in this manner to lead us logically through the various levels of our relationship with God, starting with the most emotional and spiritual, progressing to the rational, and then to the physical level. First we proclaim God one and recognize God's sovereignty over our lives. This paragraph is called *ol malchut shamayim*, the yoke of the kingdom of heaven. Then, in the second paragraph, called *ol mitzvot*, the yoke of the *mitzvot*, we affirm our relationship to God through the *mitzvot*, the commandments. Finally, we commit ourselves to expressing our relationship with God on a physical level—that is, by wearing *tsitsit*. The *tsitsit* are worn only in the daytime, since the commandment concerning them adjures us to "see" them, not to *wear* them 24 hours a day.

This order is not the one we might intuitively expect. When approaching other tasks, we usually perform them in the opposite order. Consider the example of a musician relating to a piece of music. First he or she would practice the physical aspect of simply playing the piece, and then he or she would train diligently until thoroughly familiar with each intricacy of the composition. Only then would his or her spirit be able to enter the music. The *Shema* outlines our relationship with God in the exact opposite order. We begin with the spirit, move from there to the realm of discipline, and from there to the physical plane.

Why were the paragraphs placed in this order? To emphasize the importance of our relationship with God. Judaism is primarily a relationship with God and only secondarily a set of tasks to do—that is, the *mitzvot*. The *mitzvot* serve little or no purpose unless they are an expression of our relationship with God. The assertion, commonly made, that Judaism is a religion of deed, not creed, is simply wrong.

The next mishnah considers a more serious stumbling block to intention: a lack of Jewish competence.

MISHNAH (15a): If one recites the Shema without hearing what he says, he has performed his obligation. Rabbi Jose says he has not performed his obligation.

If he recites it without pronouncing the letters correctly, Rabbi Jose says that he has performed his obligation. Rabbi Judah says that he has not performed his obligation.

If he recites it backward, he has not performed his obligation.

If he recites it and makes a mistake, he goes back to the place where he made the mistake.

GEMARA: What is Rabbi Jose's reason? Because it is written, "Hear," let your ear hear what you utter with your mouth. The first Tanna, however, explains that "Hear" means, in any language that you understand. Rabbi Jose derives both lessons from the word . . . .

GEMARA (15b): Rabbi Tavi said in the name of Rabbi Josiah, "The halachah in both cases follows the more lenient authority."

How should the *Shema* be ideally said? One should say it audibly, clearly, and with the words in the correct order. All these conditions will facilitate true intention: sincere prayer. However, the rabbis are reasonable. Not every recitation of the *Shema* will fall within these ideal parameters. So they follow the more lenient views mentioned in the mishnah.

Significantly, the rabbis label their decision as lenient. This may be construed as an injunction to be as inclusive as possible when determining the parameters of acceptable prayer practices in our own communities. Many Jews today cannot say the *Shema* fluently in Hebrew, or are hearing impaired, or have difficulty speaking, or are mentally handicapped. Yet, this *sugya* seems to indicate that if they recite the *Shema* with deep intention, it should be considered a valid recitation. This *sugya* is summarized in the accompanying diagram. The views adopted as halachah are shown in boldface.

Our third mishnah moves to a more intense kind of interference. Previously, we dealt with an external impedance to *kavanah*. In this mishnah we examine the effect of energies

Table 2–1.

		Error		
		Did not hear	Did not clearly pronounce	Improper word order
Authority	Rabbi Judah	**Fulfilled obligation**	Did not fulfill obligation	**Did not fulfill obligation**
	Rabbi Jose	Did not fulfill obligation	**Fulfilled obligation**	No comment

within us that compete with prayer—specifically, the emotions of fear, sexual arousal, and self-righteousness that can render sincere prayer impossible.

> **MISHNAH (16a):** Workmen may recite [the *Shema*] on the top of a tree or the top of a scaffolding, a thing they are not allowed to do in the case of the *Tefillah*. A bridegroom is exempt from the recital of the *Shema* from the first night [after the wedding] until the end of the Sabbath, if he has not consummated the marriage.
>
> It is told of Rabban Gamaliel that when he married, he recited the *Shema* on the first night. His students said to him, "Our teacher, you have taught us that a bridegroom is exempt from the recital of the *Shema*." He replied to them, "I will not listen to you to remove from myself the kingship of heaven even for a moment."
>
> **GEMARA:** Our Rabbis taught: Workmen may recite [the *Shema*] on the top of a tree or on the top of a scaffolding, and they may say the *Tefillah* on the top of an olive tree and the top of a fig tree, but they must come down from all other kinds of trees to the ground to pray the *Tefillah*. And the master of the house must in any case come down before saying the *Tefillah*, the reason [in all cases] being that his mind is not clear.

In this *sugya*, we continue to define what interferes with our ability to truly concentrate on the words of the *Shema*. There are some emotions so intense that they can interfere with our ability to affirm our relationship with God. Danger is one of these. While there are prayers composed especially for dangerous situations, they are requests for help, not affirmations like the *Shema*. Affirmation requires a relatively peaceful and secure state of mind.

One may recite the *Shema* in the top of a tree, while one may not recite the *Amidah* there. There may be several reasons for this ruling. First of all, the *Shema* is shorter than the *Amidah*, and therefore demands concentration for a shorter amount of time. A window washer on scaffolding off the fortieth floor of a building might be able to say the first line of the *Shema* with intention, but maintaining his concentration there over the 5 or 10 minutes it takes to recite the *Amidah* might be a more difficult act of will to perform. Second, only the first line of the *Shema* must be said with intention; but since we are asking for favor and mercy from God in the *Amidah*, we should have concentration for the whole of that prayer. Third, the Shema requires less bodily movement than does the *Amidah*, during which we stand, bow, raise ourselves on our toes, and "daven." Fourth, if a Jewish fruit picker or painter must interrupt his work twice each morning, once to say the *Shema* and again to say the *Amidah*, he might not be able to find work as easily as a non-Jewish worker, who would not impose this inconvenience on his employer.

This distinction between interrupting work for the *Amidah* and the *Shema* is reminiscent of a busy married couple's morning routine. One spouse is rushing about trying to get ready to go to work, while the other is busily doing chores around the house. As the wife runs out the door, she stops for a kiss and says to her husband, "You're my only one. I love you. See you tonight." The husband echoes her words, something of a ritual with them, since this scenario is repeated each weekday morning. If they intend to have a longer conversation, they'll have to put aside their other concerns, sit down, and focus on each other. The first exchange is analogous to the *Shema*—an affirmation, perhaps quickly said, but deeply felt. The *Amidah* is like the extended conversation that requires a more tranquil atmosphere.

Sexual arousal is another major emotion that can interfere with our concentration. When a man was about to consummate his love for the first time, the rabbis accepted that he would not be able to say the *Shema* with the required intention, so they exempted the bridegroom from the obligation to say the *Shema* on his wedding night. Of course, the rabbis felt that the bride was not obligated to say the *Shema* at any time.

The rabbis seem to be acknowledging that we must be in touch with our romantic, and even sexual, feelings for God if we are to pray with true intention. On a man's wedding night, none of this energy would be available to be channeled into the relationship with God; it would all be focused on his new wife. Therefore, the rabbis recognize that his prayer could not be sincerely and completely felt.

Later Jewish thinkers explicitly stated the role of sexuality in their relationship with God. Maimonides says in the *Mishneh Torah*, "[The love of God is a love] so strong that one's soul shall be knit up with it, and one should be continually enraptured by it, like a love-sick man, whose mind is at no time free from his passion for a woman; the thought of her filling his heart at all times, when sitting down or rising up, when eating or drinking" (*Sefer HaMadah, Hilchot Teshuvah*, 10:5).

Rabban Gamaliel's behavior demonstrates another kind of obstacle to true prayer: the extreme piety that can turn into self-righteousness. He rather arbitrarily decided that the exemption from saying the *Shema* on his wedding night did not apply to him. Gamaliel deviated from Jewish practice to express his extreme piety at several other times in his life as well. For example, he mourned his slave, and he washed himself while in deep mourning for his wife. Both of these actions are normally forbidden. Piety, of course, can be a very positive force in our relationship with God, as we will see in Chapter 5. When it is tainted with self-righteousness, however, piety can actually interfere with that relationship.

In general, the rabbis held a balanced view of our relationship with God. They understood that certain feelings, such as fear or sexual arousal, will sometimes compete within us for energy for that relationship. As long as these situations are recognized and dealt with, they will not pose a threat to the core relationship. However, attempts at extreme piety such as Rabban Gamaliel's are truly a threat: if we can't admit that there are times when we are not relating to God, then we are not living the rest of our lives fully, as the rabbis wanted us to do.

The Gemara defines Heaven as a place without interferences with our relationship with God.

GEMARA (17a): A favorite saying of Rav was, "[The World to Come is not like this world.] In the World to Come there is no eating nor drinking nor propagation nor business nor jealousy nor hatred nor competition, but the righteous sit with their crowns on their heads feasting on the brightness of the Divine Presence."

Here we see how important it is to understand the context of any given piece of Talmud. If we did not know that this chapter was defining, and dealing with, interferences in our basic relationship with God, we would think that this was simply a charming free association placed here for no particular reason. Within our context, however, we can see that Rav defines the future world as one where all the things that interfere with our basic relationship with God are absent. For Rav, Paradise is being able to relate to God directly, continuously, and without interruption.

Rav's comment, and others throughout the Talmud, form the basis of the Jewish view of the afterlife. However, there is no definitive description of life after death in Judaism. There is a pleasant place called *Olam HaBah*, the World to Come, and an unpleasant place called *Gehinnom*, but there is little agreement about the nature of these realms, nor is great emphasis placed on exact definitions of them.

Our chapter now progresses to the topic of what the rabbis considered permanent obstacles to our relationship with God.

> **GEMARA (17a):** Greater is the promise made by the Holy One, Blessed be He, to the women than to the men, for it says, "Rise up, you women that are at ease; you confident daughters, give ear unto my speech" (Isaiah 32:9). Rav said to R. Hiyya, "Whereby do women earn merit? By taking their children to synagogue [to learn Scripture] and sending their husbands to the Beit HaMidrash [to learn Mishnah], and waiting until they return from the Beit HaMidrash.

This *sugya* deals with a different kind of interference that prevents one from reciting the Shema with the required intention. In the rabbis' view, being a woman interfered with one's ability to relate to God. They assumed that a woman was responsible for the demanding, and time-consuming, tasks of raising children and managing a household and therefore could not be held responsible for performing positive, time-bound commandments; the category shown in boldface in the accompanying diagram.

Examples of the various categories of *mitzvot* are as follows:

Table 2-2.

Commandments

	Time-bound	Not time-bound
Positive	**Women not obligated**	Women are obligated
Negative	Women are obligated	Women are obligated

1. *Positive, time-bound commandments:* Things we are to do only at certain times, such as saying the *Shema* and wearing the *tallit*.
2. *Positive, not-time-bound commandments*: Things we are to do and do all the time, such as honoring our parents and loving our neighbor as ourselves.
3. *Negative, not-time-bound commandments*: Things we are to refrain from doing at all times, such as murdering, bearing false witness, and stealing.
4. *Negative, time-bound commandments*: Things we must refrain from doing only at certain times, such as not eating bread on Passover, not working on Shabbat, and not eating on Yom Kippur.

There are many exceptions to the rules of this system. Women are, in fact, obligated to perform some positive, time-bound commandments, such as lighting the candles on Hannukah. Women are not *forbidden* to perform positive time-bound commandments; they are simply *not obligated* to do most of them. (See Chapter 7 for the numerous exceptions to these rules.) They may perform these *mitzvot* voluntarily if they wish to do so.

Because women are not *obligated* to do these *mitzvot*, the rabbis ruled that women cannot have the same intention and sense of responsibility regarding the *mitzvot* as do men. The following example may clarify this concept. Imagine that Joe and Ted each owe Fred 10 dollars. Today is Monday. They must each repay the 10 dollars by Friday or pay a 50 percent fine. Sue does not owe Fred any money. She volunteers to collect the men's money and deliver it to Fred. The men refuse, fearing that, since she does not owe any money herself and is not liable to any fine, she may forget to make the delivery. Joe and Ted represent Jewish men in this system of *mitzvot*; Sue represents a Jewish woman's role, and the debt owed is the positive, time-bound commandments. Given this system, women can never function as *shelichot tsibbur*—persons who may perform a *mitzvah* on someone else's behalf in a traditional Jewish community. (Although women cannot lead a congregation of men and women in prayer, there is some dispute within the traditional community over whether women may lead a service at which no men are present.)

Some critics of this system contend that it is sexist and designed to exclude women from public religious life. Some traditional thinkers answer that this system was devised to *help* women by lessening the claims made on their already overcommitted time; the "mommy-track" for *mitzvot*, as it were. They also contend that raising children is so spiritually elevating that women have less need of prayer.

Both groups of thinkers make valid points. There is no denying that the rabbis simply did not consider women full participants in Jewish religious life. In part, this is because they made assumptions about women's roles that no longer hold true. We no longer assume that women are the primary caretakers of home and children, or even that they want to be married and have children. The burdens that the rabbis assumed that women carried are now often not carried at all, shouldered by others, or shared with a spouse. On the other hand, raising children *is* spiritually elevating. However, it is just as elevating for men as it is for women. It is interesting that the rabbis did not suggest that men spend more time with their children as a means to come closer with God.

In our foregoing text, women are clearly seen as enablers, not as persons who perform *mitzvot* in their own right. Women are rewarded for enabling their children and husbands to study Torah, not for studying Torah themselves. However, the more women study Torah, the more genuinely committed they will be to sharing it with those they love. Helping someone else study Torah without studying it oneself is like trying to enthusiastically urge them to eat something you've never tasted. Your exhortations may be effective, but they will be even *more* effective, and more sincere expressions of your love, if you know the sweetness your loved ones are about to enjoy.

3

What Happens When the Holy Meets the Profane?

I magine that you are helping a good friend with her wedding. Everything has been planned down to the smallest detail to ensure that this day will be special, different from all others. Random accidents will not mar the beauty of the day. Then, 10 minutes before the wedding is to begin, the flower girl spills cranberry juice all over the front of the bride's dress. How do you handle the situation? How do you reclaim the purity, the specialness of that dress? These are the sorts of situations (although more intense and serious) that the rabbis explore in this chapter.

The theme of this chapter flows naturally from that of the previous one. We move from dealing with the things that interfere with our relationship with God to things that might destroy it. This is framed as a problem of the meeting of the *kodesh* (holy) and *chol* (profane). *Kodesh* is used here to indicate, not items belonging to the ancient Temple, but the everyday holiness of righteousness and piety—states of true, deep connection with God. *Chol* includes emotions and states that threaten to disrupt our relationship with God, such as intense grief, having too many demands on our time, or contact with excrement.

A subset of *kodesh* is the category *tahara*, ritual purity. A subset of chol is *tumah*, ritual impurity. (There are three main sources of ritual impurity: death, disease [e.g., leprosy], and sexual functions [e.g., seminal emissions or menstrual blood].)

A spectrum running from most intense profaneness to most intense holiness might look like this:

Tumah———Chol———/———Kodesh———Taharah

This relationship between profaneness and impurity may be easier to understand if we take the opposite case. Purity is a kind of holiness, but it is not the only kind. For example, one can achieve holiness by performing acts of loving kindness or by observing the *mitzvot*.

The profane is a legitimate part of life: we even affirm it as such when we say the blessing over the end of Shabbat (*Havdalah*). The profane need not be something negative, but simply something that cannot be clearly classified as holy. The rabbis were not trying to eradicate profaneness. They simply wanted to deal with its effects on our lives. They did *not* advocate that we retreat from the secular, nonholy aspects of life: monasticism has *rarely* found a place in mainstream Jewish thought.

The material in this chapter may embarrass us or make us feel uncomfortable. Why did the rabbis spend so much time discussing urination and defecation? How is this material holy? Why should we study this chapter today? These passages are relevant when we see these issues as vehicles for examining the broader concepts just mentioned.

If the rabbis had been examining the meeting of the holy and profane today, they might have couched it in terms of a set of *tefillin* that was mistakenly taken to the city dump or was found in a drug-infested apartment building. (*Tefillin* serve as an especially good vehicle to explore these issues, since they can easily be carried into the world, away from the synagogue.) Think about how you feel when you come in contact with something or someone evil or impure. Don't you want to cleanse yourself and restore yourself to the state you were in before you had that contact? This is the issue the rabbis are addressing. The solution they propose is based on using our minds to create an inner state of holiness and purity that can overcome the forces outside us. *Kavanah*, intention, is here used for more than concentrating on communicating with God through prayer, as was advocated in Chapter 2. Here, the rabbis show us how to use our inner concentration to shut out those things that interfere with our prayer *or* acknowledge that the distraction is too great for even inner concentration to overcome. Then they permit us to stop trying to pray.

Confronting death is the most potent example of this phenomenon. If one attends a funeral in order to comfort a mourner, one is exempt from saying the *Shema*: one's inner state will not allow a genuine recital of prayer. However, if one attends simply to see the crowd, and is not affected on an inner level, one must say the *Shema*, since there is no genuine contact with the profane. (It is ironic that if one cares about the dead and their mourners, they are influenced by the profane; if they do not care, they are not.)

> **MISHNAH (17b)**: One whose dead [relative] lies before him is exempt from the recital of the *Shema* and from the *Tefillah* and from *Tefillin* and from all the precepts laid down in the Torah. . . . When they have buried the dead and returned [from the grave], if they have time to begin and finish [the *Shema*] before forming a row, they should begin. But if not, they should not begin. Of those who stand in the row, those on the inside are exempt, but those on the outside are not exempt.

The first mishnah of this chapter begins with the most basic, and most intense, form of the profane: death. The rabbis recognized that someone who is mourning will not be able to summon the intention needed for sincere prayer. They are still devoting too much energy trying to be connected with the deceased to make a connection with God.

After the funeral, it was customary for those who had attended the service to precede the mourners to their home. There they formed parallel lines between which the mourners could walk and receive condolences. At this point in the mourning process, the exemptions from saying the *Shema* are restricted. One may say the *Shema* if there is enough time to do so before the mourners arrive. However, when in the presence of their grief, a legitimate kind of profanity, one would have difficulty making contact with the holy (God). Their grief is the opposite of the passionate love of God and life that the rabbis are promoting in this tractate. Therefore, those who actually

face the mourners and offer their condolences will not be able
to say the *Shema* as they should. Those who do not have direct
contact with the mourners may be able to recite the *Shema*
properly.

Proximity to mourners depends not only on physical nearness but also on psychological nearness:

> **GEMARA (19b):** "Those who stand in a row, etc." Our Rab-
> bis taught, "The row which can see inside is exempt, but one
> which cannot see inside is not exempt." Rabbi Judah says,
> "Those who come on account of the mourner are exempt, but
> those who come for their own purposes are not exempt."

Physical *and* emotional proximity to the mourners, and
their grief, exempts one from having to say the *Shema*. It is
one's *inner* state that enables one to made a connection with
God or with mourners.

The rabbis attribute great power to grief. It extends beyond the mourners to those around them, almost as if the
mourners were radioactive and their "fallout" affected those
nearest them. When truly empathizing with a mourner, we can
take a bit of their pain into ourselves: this is how we help them.
It takes a tremendous amount of energy to absorb such pain.
Comforting mourners in this way is one of the greatest *mitzvot*
in the Jewish tradition. Therefore, the rabbis exempt us from
relating to God while we are engaged in it, and they authorize
us to use our energy for this *mitzvah*. It's as if God is saying, "I
know you're not ignoring me. You're just helping out someone
in need. I'll still be here when you're finished."

By exempting us from saying the *Shema*, the rabbis are apparently authorizing a "violation" of the Torah. After all, the
Torah commands us to say the *Shema* morning and evening
with no exceptions. The sages endowed the system of *mitzvot*
with great flexibility that enables us to make choices within that
system. Consider, for example, the principle *Haoseik b'mitzvah
patur min ha-mitzvah*, "One who is engaged in one *mitzvah* can
be exempted from the obligation to perform another *mitzvah*."
Here they clearly put the needs of other people in dire straits
above our need to relate to God. Thus, we see once more that

maintaining relationships is of paramount importance in Judaism.

However, there is also a time to let go of relationships. Once someone has died, we must turn our energies to the living and to God. If we believed that the dead could be active in our lives as a supernatural power independent of God, then we might channel some of our intensity into relating to them rather than into relating to God. Their continued influence in our lives would result in less contact with the holy, clearly an undesirable result. Yet it is difficult to give up relationships with people once they have died. The following story expresses this tension within the Jewish tradition.

> **GEMARA (18b:** It has been taught: it is related that a certain pious man gave a dinar to a poor man on the eve of New Year in a year of drought, and his wife scolded him, and he went and passed the night in the cemetery, and he heard two spirits conversing with one another.
>
> Said one to her companion: " My dear, come and let us wander about the world and let us hear from behind the curtain what suffering is coming on the world."
>
> Said her companion to her, "I am not able, because I am buried in a matting of reeds. But do you go, and whatever you hear, tell me." So the other went and wandered about and returned. Said her companion to her, "My dear, what have you heard from behind the curtain?"
>
> She replied, "I heard that whoever sows after the first rainfall will have his crop smitten by hail." So the man went and did not sow till after the second rainfall, with the result that everyone else's crop was smitten and his was not smitten.
>
> The next year, he again went and passed the night in the cemetery, and heard the two spirits conversing with one another. Said one to her companion, "Come and let us wander about the world and hear from behind the curtain what punishment is coming upon the world."
>
> Said the other to her, "My dear, did I not tell you that I am not able because I am buried in a matting of reeds? But do you go, and whatever you hear, come and tell me." So the other one went and wandered about the world and returned.
>
> She said to her, "My dear, what have you heard from behind the curtain?"

She replied, "I heard that whoever sows after the later rain will have his crop smitten with blight."

So the man went and sowed after the first rain with the result that everyone else's crop was blighted and his was not blighted.

Said his wife to him, "How is it that last year everyone else's crop was smitten and yours was not smitten, and this year everyone else's crop is blighted and yours is not blighted?" So he related to her all his experiences.

The story goes that a few days later, a quarrel broke out between the wife of that pious man and the mother of the [dead] child [buried in the reeds], and the former said to the latter, "Come and I will show you your daughter buried in a matting of reeds."

The next year the man again went and spent the night in the cemetery and heard the spirits conversing together.

One said, "My dear, come and let us wander about the world and hear from behind the curtain what suffering is coming upon the world."

Said the other, "My dear, let me be. The words [spoken] between you and me have been heard among the living." This would prove they [the dead] know? Perhaps some other man after his decease went and told them.

This story is composed to show that God controls everything, both while we live and after we die. The action in the story begins with an act of *tsedakah*, charity, on the eve of the Jewish New Year, the time when God notes our actions and rewards and punishes us for them. The protagonist gives a coin to a poor man in a year of drought. In other words, at a very busy time, in pressed circumstances, this man was able to help his fellow. For this, God rewards him. His wife's scolding him is simply the mechanism God uses to bring him to the cemetery so he can hear the information he will need to earn his reward. The man hears two spirits talking to each other. (Steinsaltz [1983] explains that souls are linked to their corpses until they disintegrate.) One of the spirits was ashamed, for she had been buried in shrouds made of reeds, the poorest possible material. Therefore, her spirit stays behind while the other spirit hears God's will from behind the curtain that screens the Divine Presence from the world. The man's wife also serves as the instrument God uses to bring the tale to its close, when the protagonist has received a sufficient reward for his charity. In other words, God is controlling everyone—the man, his wife, and the spirits—in order to effect a reward for righteousness.

This story is part of a larger section in which the rabbis try to determine how the dead relate to the living. They were anxious to dispel any superstitious notions that the dead can hear us or have any effect on our lives. Why? Because if people believed this, then they might take some, and possibly much, of the intensity they should be putting into their relationship with God and channel it into relating to the deceased, almost praying to *them* rather than to God, to fix things in their lives. However, this story represents a strong superstitious tradition that the rabbis could not extinguish: the belief that the dead influence our lives and that we could profit from their knowledge if we could but obtain it. The rabbis reject this notion. Even the *spirits* seem to reject the idea. In the end, the spirits realize that they have been overheard and feel that their influence on the lives of the living is improper. But how did they realize that they had been overheard? Was it through contact with the living? No. Someone who had died between the second and third incidents came and told them. Therefore, there was no direct contact between the dead and the living.

The Gemara states this in explicit terms:

> **GEMARA (19a):** Rabbi Isaac said, "If one makes remarks about the dead, it is like making remarks about a stone." Some say [the reason is that] they do not know, others that they know but do not care. Can that be so? Has not Rav Papa said, "A certain man made derogatory remarks about Mar Samuel and a log fell from the roof and broke his skull"? A [Torah] scholar is different, because the Holy One blessed be He, avenges his insult [Himself].

How ambivalent the rabbis were about this issue! Some things in their world must have been inexplicable to them save for the influence of the dead, demons, and spirits. So, for instance, here, Rabbi Isaac states flatly that the dead do not hear us. But apparently a man had insulted Samuel after his death and was injured by a log falling from a roof. The Gemara then explains that it is not the deceased, but God, who avenged the insult. Steinsaltz (1983) in summarizing the *halachah* on this point, indicates that it is a *Beit Din*, a Jewish court, that judges the slanderer and compels him to do *teshuvah* for the offense. Thus, the later commentators continue the sages' tendency to minimize the dead's influence in our lives.

As the rabbis examine the contact of the holy and the profane, they continue to clarify the definition of the holy in us. They ask why miracles are no longer performed in their generation, even though they are more learned than former generations.

> **GEMARA (20a):** Said Rav Papa to Abaye, "How were former generations different from ours and so merited that miracles were performed for them and miracles are not performed for us? It cannot be because of their [superiority in] study, because in the years of Rav Judah the whole of their studies was confined to *Nezikin*, and we study all six orders, and when Rav Judah came in [the tractate] *Ukzin* [to the law] 'If a woman pressed vegetables in a pot' . . . he used to say, 'I see all the difficulties of Rav and Samuel here,' and we have thirteen versions of *Ukzin*. And yet when Rav Judah drew off one shoe, rain used to come, whereas we torment ourselves and cry loudly, and no notice is taken of us!"
>
> He replied, "The former generations used to be ready to sacrifice their lives for the sanctification of [God's] name; we do not sacrifice our lives for the sanctification of [God's] name."

"Why are miracles not performed for us?" the *Amoraim* wondered. Their puzzlement centers on their erudition. Apparently, in their minds, study of Mishnah was the surest way to come close to God. In this *sugya*, they seem to question that supposition. Instead, they begin to understand that it is devotion and commitment that best build a relationship with God, *not* intellectual acumen. Even Talmud, if studied only with one's mind, and not with one's heart and soul and *life*, will not produce the intense, intimate relationship with God that the rabbis advocated. These rabbis were learned, but they were not willing to make intense contact with the most profane (death) for the sake of the most holy (God).

The deepest—some would say mystic—relationship with God may lead us toward the edge of the greatest profaneness. There is a famous story about four rabbis who entered the "garden," considered by many to be a euphemism for "mystical speculation" on page 14b of the tractate *Hagigah*.

GEMARA (Hagigah 14b): Our Rabbis taught: Four men entered the Garden, namely, Ben Azzai and Ben Zoma, Aher and Rabbi Akiba.... Ben Azzai cast a look and died... Ben Zoma looked and became demented... Aher mutilated the shoots. Rabbi Akiba departed unhurt.

Only Rabbi Akiba survived this intense spiritual encounter intact. Of the other three, one went mad, one turned to idol worship, and one died on the spot. Why did Rabbi Akiba survive? Because he was willing to sacrifice himself for God's name, as we will see by his martyr's death, in Chapter 9. Because he had this strength, this miracle was performed for him: he entered a realm of danger and death and left intact. He was able to find holiness in what others found profane.

In our next *sugya*, the rabbis attempt to define the relationship of women, children, and slaves to God. The sages see these persons as *chol*, outside the realm of holiness.

MISHNAH (20a): Women, slaves, and minors are exempt form reciting the Shema (20b) and [putting on] Tefillin, but are obligated to [say] the *Tefillah*, [put up a] mezuzah and [say] grace after meals.

GEMARA: That they are exempt from the Shema is self-evident. It is a positive mitzvah for which there is a fixed time and women are exempt from all positive mitzvot for which there is a fixed time. You might say that because it mentions the kingship of heaven it is different. We are therefore told that this is not so.

"And from [putting on] the *Tefillin*." This is also self-evident. You might say that because it is juxtaposed in the Torah with the mezuzah [and therefore women would be subject to it]. Therefore we are told that this is not so.

"They are subject to the obligation of *Tefillah*." Because this [is a supplication for Divine] mercy. You might think that because it is written in connection with [the *Tefillah*], "Evening and morning and at noonday (Psalms 55:18)," that it is like a positive mitz-

vah for which there is a fixed time. Therefore we are told that
this is not so.

"And mezuzah." This is self-evident. You might say that because it is juxtaposed in the Torah with the study of the Torah,
[therefore women would be exempt]. Therefore it tells us that
this is not so.

"And grace after meals." This is self-evident—You might
think that because it is written, "When the Lord shall give you
in the evening flesh to eat and in the morning bread to the full
(Exodus 16:8)," therefore it is like a positive mitzvah for which
there is a definite time. Therefore it tells us that this is not so . . .

A son may say grace on behalf of his father and a slave may
say grace on behalf of his master and a woman may say grace on
behalf of her husband. But the sages said, "A curse come upon
the man whose wife and children say grace for him."

Women, children, and slaves may communicate with
God, but they are not obligated to affirm the *core* relationship
by saying the *Shema* and wearing *tefillin*, presumably because
they do not participate fully in this core relationship. Women,
slaves, and minors may petition God for mercy (the *tefillah*),
they may witness God's presence as they enter their homes
(*mezuzah*), and they may thank God for the food they eat (grace
after meals). But they do not affirm the basic relationship with
word (reciting the *Shema*) or body (wearing *tefillin*). Clearly,
they are seen as having a less direct or less immediate relationship with God than do free adult men. To the rabbis, it seemed
that women, children, and slaves all were handicapped in their
ability to join the chain of tradition by studying and teaching
Torah. They claimed that women did not have the time, children were not sufficiently intellectually developed, and slaves
did not have either the time or the opportunity because of their
station in life.

One explanation of this *sugya* involves the married couple
we met in Chapter 2. The wife was rushing out the door, but
affirmed her relationship with her husband as she did so. Now
imagine their children, an aunt, and a housekeeper are watch-
ing this interchange. By virtue of this marriage, these bystanders have a house and food and work. The children, aunt,
and housekeeper do not participate in the direct relationship

between husband and wife, but their well-being depends on that relationship flourishing, and they are grateful that it does. Each of them also has his own, less intimate, relationship with the husband and wife. The bystanders represent children, women, and slaves: the wife stands for free adult men, and the husband represents God.

The rabbis show, by the way they manipulate the categories of positive, negative, time-bound, and not-time-bound *mitzvot*, that these are not the true criteria for determining how women, slaves, and children may relate to God. It would seem clear that the *tefillah* is a positive, time-bound commandment, just like the *Shema*. However, the rabbis do not define it as such, for they did not want to cut off all means of communication between God and women, minors, and slaves. The sages created a system that defines these persons out of the most intense, basic relationship with God, but acknowledges that they do have *some* kind of relationship with the Deity.

The final line of this *sugya* can be read as a strong encouragement to free adult men to become Jewishly competent. They should be role models of piety for their wives, children, and slaves. However, this interpretation assumes that women, children, and slaves are incapable of maintaining a direct relationship with God on the same level as grown men. Indeed, it ignores the possibility that these groups of people might be able to legitimately teach free, grown men something about that relationship.

On the other hand, with this line, the *Amoraim* may be reminding grown, free men that they need to say prayers *more* than do these other classes of people. All three of these types of persons experienced powerlessness in some way. They knew that they did not completely control their lives, and so they may have readily looked to God for direction. But grown, free men might be tempted to believe that the world is in their control, that they owed God nothing. So it is *they* who need prayer more than anyone else. Note, however, that this interpretation does not eliminate the inherent sexism of this *sugya*: it simply changes its target!

Torah study is a key to maintaining the basic relationship with God, and anything that might interrupt this activity, such as ritual impurity, must be minimized.

> **GEMARA (22a):** Those with venereal disease, lepers, and those who had intercourse with *niddot* are permitted to read the Torah, the Prophets and the Writings, and to study the Mishnah, the Talmud, halachot and aggadot, but *ba'alei keri* are forbidden [to do so] . . . Words of Torah are not susceptible to ritual impurity.

In this *sugya*, the rabbis show us how to deal with the two other major sources of impurity besides death: those resulting from sexual functions (venereal disease, seminal emission, and menstruation) and disease (leprosy). Those men who had gonorrhea or leprosy or had intercourse with a menstruating woman are allowed to study Torah. But a *ba'al keri*, one who had a seminal emission (through masturbation or sexual intercourse) is restricted in what he may study. It was thought that one could have a seminal emission only from *kalut rosh*, lightheadedness. Such an emission implied that the *ba'al keri* was insufficiently serious or dignified. He was unable to remember his relationship with God at all times, for cognizance of this relationship would have prevented such behavior.

The rabbis tended to permit ritually impure persons to study Torah if they did not become defiled through "lightheadedness." These persons were allowed to study the vast majority of Jewish texts, as long as they did not mention God's name while in an impure state. The rabbis wanted to minimize interference in communication with God, even for those in a state of ritual impurity. A person in that state would be uplifted by the words of Torah.

Over the years, the rabbis gradually diminished the observance of the laws of impurity and purity. Today, all Jews are presumed to be ritually impure, although members of the priestly family of Cohanim are forbidden to make contact with a corpse even today. Some Hasidic sects have reintroduced the duty of bathing in the *mikveh* for one who had a seminal emission, and observant women go to the *mikveh* to purify themselves after each menstrual period.

The waters of the *mikveh* are a vehicle for changing an individual's status in Judaism. If one enters the water impure in body, mind, or soul, one leaves it having regained one's neutral status. Of one enters in a neutral state (such as before one's wedding), one leaves the waters imbued with extra holiness, as illustrated here.

	mikveh		*mikveh*	
negative state	→	**neutral state**	→	**positive state**
(impure) (−)		(0)		(pure) (+)

The *mikveh* has great power even today. It can be used as a status changer and it can also be a pleasant, and powerful, experience. Some men immerse themselves in it every Friday afternoon so that they can greet Shabbat in a state of extra holiness. All Jews, not just traditional ones, may use the *mikveh* when they feel impure.

The categories of *tahara* and *tumah*, ritual purity and impurity, and the way in which they interfere with our relationship with God, may be difficult for us to understand. One way to comprehend this concept might be to imagine that you are in great pain *and* trying to maintain a treasuring relationship with another person. For instance, a woman who is having a contraction during labor might want to relate to her husband but might be overwhelmed by the pain she is experiencing. Once the contraction is over, she will be able to speak to her husband and relate to him quite well. Similarly, when we are in the deep emotional pain of depression, we may want to be close to our loved ones, but we may not be able to relate fully to them. In both cases the relationship at the moment of contact may be tinged with pain. Ritual impurity is like that pain: it interferes with our ability to relate to God because something is awry within ourselves.

While our human relationships can be spoiled by impurity or pain, our relationship with God through Torah is impervious to this influence. The words of Torah cannot be defiled. If we read them when we are depressed or in pain, they can only lift us up. We cannot drag the words of Torah down.

Our inner state of mind is the most potent force in our ability to make contact with God and truly maintain a holy state when surrounded by the profane.

GEMARA (23a): Our rabbis taught: One who enters a regular privy takes off his *tefillin* at a distance of four cubits and puts them in the window on the side of the public way and enters, and when he comes out he goes a distance of four cubits and puts them on. These are the words of Beit Shammai.

Beit Hillel says, "He holds them in his hand and enters."

Rabbi Akiba said, "He holds them in his garment and enters."

Did it occur to you to say, "In his garment"? Sometimes they might slip out and fall! Say rather, he holds them in his garment and in his hand, and enters, and he puts them in a hole next to the privy, but he should not put them in a hole close to the public way, lest they should be taken by passers-by, and he should render himself suspect. It is told of one student who placed his *tefillin* in a hole next to the public way, and a prostitute came and took them. And she went to the to the Beit HaMidrash and said, "See what this man gave me for my hire!" And when the student heard this, he went to the top of a roof and fell and died. Thereupon they ordained that a man should hold them in his garment and in his hand and then go in.

The power of an inner state of holiness to overcome physical contact with the profane is found in the laws concerning *tefillin* in a privy. In ancient days, *tefillin* were worn all day long, not just at worship services, as they are now. Therefore, one had to cope with the possibility that the holiness of the *tefillin* might make contact with the profane—in this case, human excrement. (Note that excrement is not ritually impure.) Ideally, one should physically separate the holy and the profane. In this *sugya*, they recommend a distance of 4 cubits (approximately 7 feet). But where this endangers life, mental separation is enough. Again, one's inward state is the determining factor in maintaining holiness.

The rabbis almost always seek to empower us, giving us ways to keep ourselves holy and in contact with God, and giving us the means to return to holiness if we have been in contact with the profane. Therefore, they legitimize the power of our minds to keep us separate and holy. Holiness can be engendered, and maintained, in every individual.

4

Prayer and Personalities

T he words "I love you" are seldom accompanied by the word "please." That is because "I love you" is an affirmation not a request. However, in the best relationships, including our relationship with God, we express not only love for the other, but our very selves, and our needs, comfortably. This is the topic the rabbis proceed to explore in this chapter.

Now that the rabbis have defined our basic relationship with God, they move on to what we usually think of as prayer: affirming our relationship with, while requesting things from, God. The next two chapters cover the *Amidah*, the prayer par excellence in Judaism, which is said three times each day. Like a character in a Russian novel, this prayer goes by several names. The *Amidah* (Standing) is also called the *Tefillah* (Prayer) and the *Shemoneh Esrei* (Eighteen Benedictions). We can think of this prayer as being an appliance with detachable parts. You use the basic appliance, adding various attachments as you need them. In the *Amidah*, the "basic appliance"—that is, the things we always have—are the first three blessings and the last three blessings. The section in between is the variable one, the "attachment."

In the first section of this prayer we approach God. The *Avot* (Fathers), the first prayer in this section, reminds God that we are related to great Jews of the past. We pray that through *their* merit, if not our own, God will listen to our prayers. In the next prayer, *Gevurot* (Mightiness) we praise God's power to resurrect the dead. The third blessing, *Kedushat HaShem* (sanctification of God's name) declares God to be holy. Then, on weekdays, we proceed to petition God for the things we want. These requests are listed in the middle section in the following outline. The first five blessings in this section, in italics, are personal requests. The last eight requests are petitions for the needs of the Jewish people. Schurer (1986), in his classic work, relates these communal petitions to what the Jews of the rabbinic era hoped would be the historical development of the messianic era. He notes that the tenth benediction calls for the ingathering of the exiles; the eleventh, for the reinstatement of national authority; the twelfth and thirteenth, for justice administered by that authority; the fourteenth, for the rebuilding of Jerusalem; the fifteenth, for the sending of the son of David (i.e., the messiah) and the establishment of his kingdom; and finally, the seventeenth, for the restoration of sacrificial worship in Jerusalem (p. 152).

Like the first three blessings, we recite the last three each time we say the *Amidah*. In these blessings, having made our requests, we take our leave of God, so to speak. The first of these blessings, *Retsei* (please accept), asks God to accept the prayers and petitions we have just offered. *Hoda'ah* (thanks) is just that: an expression of thanks to God. *Shalom Rav* (great peace) said in the afternoon and evening, and *Sim Shalom* (grant us peace), said in the morning, close the *Amidah*. Why a different prayer for morning and evening? Both prayers were part of the tradition, and the compilers of the prayer book did not want to exclude either version. Prayers for special occasions are added at various points in the *Amidah*, as here indicated.

Structure of the Amidah

1. Avot
2. Gevurot
3. Kedushat HaShem

Weekday Petitions

Individual Petitions

4. *Understanding (Havdalah)*
5. *Repentance*
6. *Forgiveness*
7. *Redemption (Prayer for Fast Days)*
8. *Healing*

Communal Petitions

9. The Blessing of the Year (for food)
10. Ingathering of the Exiles
11. The Return of Justice
12. Minim (Heretics)
13. Tsadikim (Righteous Ones)
14. Building of Jerusalem
15. Messiah son of David
16. Hearken to Prayer

OR

Shabbat

Shabbat and Creation (Friday evening)
Shabbat and Revelation (Saturday morning)
Shabbat and the Temple Cult (Musaf, Saturday morning)
Shabbat and Redemption (Saturday afternoon)

AND/OR

Festivals

Various insertions
17. Retsei
(Intermediate days of a festival)
18. Hoda'ah
(Chanukah)
(Purim)
19. Shalom Rav (evening and afternoon)
Sim Shalom (morning)

The *Amidah* differs from the *Shema* in two very important ways. First, the *Shema* is a recital of verses from the Torah, a ritual statement of love and fidelity. Its only purpose is to affirm our relationship with God. The *Amidah*, on the other hand, is an expression of our love for God *and* a plea for divine mercy. The difference between the two prayers can be likened to an unqualified, deeply felt "I love you" and an equally deeply felt "I love you and need something from you." Second, the *Amidah* is a dictate of the rabbis, *DeRabbanan*. Its recital is not derived from the Torah, *DeOraita*, as is the recital of the *Shema*. For this reason, the rabbis had many decisions to make regarding the *Amidah* that were not even issues where the *Shema* was concerned: how it should be said, what body motions should accompany its recital, and so forth. The rabbis' personalities, and their attitudes toward prayer, are revealed in the process of their deliberations of these issues. It is this interaction of prayer and personality that is this chapter's theme.

Although there are many theories regarding the origins of the *Tefillah*, one seems to have gained general acceptance. Many scholars, Steinsaltz (1983), among them, believe that the *Tefillot* were said while the Temple still stood. According to Schurer (1986), the priests followed a rotating schedule of twenty-four "courses" in which they performed their priestly duties for a week. These priests derived economic gain from officiating at the Temple because they were allowed to keep certain portions of every sacrifice for themselves and their families. (Schurer's explanation and description of the Temple cult are well worth reading.) While the priests from a certain region officiated in Jerusalem, the communities from which they came held simultaneous prayer services in their *beit haK'neset*, their synagogue. An analogous situation today would be a delegation from North Dakota coming to Washington to meet the president. At the same time as the delegation's appointment, its supporters would hold a rally at home.

We begin our examination of the *Amidah* just as we began our discussion of the *Shema*: with a definition of *when* it should be said.

MISHNAH (26a): The morning *Tefillah* [can be said] until midday. Rabbi Judah says till the fourth hour. The afternoon Tefillah [can be said] till the evening. Rabbi Judah says until the middle of the afternoon. The evening prayer has no fixed limit.

The time for the Additional Prayers is the whole of the day. Rabbi Judah says, till the seventh hour.

This mishnah shows that the rabbis who organized the Talmud were using the chronology of a day as one of their organizing factors when they composed this tractate. The discussion of the *Shema* began with its evening recitation, since this is the first one of the day. Why, then, do we begin our discussion with the morning *Amidah*, not the evening one? This issue will be addressed more fully in a moment, but suffice it to say that the morning *Amidah* is the first one of the day that is absolutely required by Jewish law. Note, too, that whereas the discussion of the *Shema* begins with the question *"from* when?" the discussion of the *Amidah* begins with the question *"till* when?" This seems to connote less of a sense of urgency about saying the *Amidah* at a specific time than about saying the *Shema*.

As we noted in Chapter 1, the system of counting time in the ancient world was quite different from ours. Each day and night was divided into 12 variable hours, regardless of the season. Therefore, the length of an hour depended on the season of the year. The law followed the opinions in boldface in the following table.

Why did Rabbi Judah assign more restrictive time limits for the *Tefillot* than the majority of rabbis? There is a penchant within the Jewish legal-religious system for exact measurements, and this ruling may simply be part of that proclivity. Rabbi Judah may also have wanted to make "a fence around

	Morning	Afternoon	Evening	Musaf
Anonymous	till midday	till evening	**no fixed limit**	all day
Rabbi Judah	**till fourth hour**	**till middle of afternoon**	no opinion recorded	**till seventh hour**

the Torah" (*Pirkei Avot* 1:1) and prevent people from feeling that they had so much leeway that they delayed saying the *Tefillah* until it was too late. Most important, he linked the timing of the *Tefillot* to the timing of the sacrifices, whereas the anonymous majority did not do so to the same extent.

The form in which this mishnah is written underscores this chapter's theme of the interaction of prayer and personality. In this mishnah, one individual holds sway over the anonymous majority. This is unusual. This connection with the chapter's theme is supported by one additional fact. The nature of the evening *Tefillah*, first broached in this mishnah, was the topic of a famous interaction of personality and prayer: a fight between Rabban Gamaliel and Rabbi Joshua (the *sugya* from page 27b). All the characters in this story are early *Tannaim*. It seems likely that this tale was well known to Rabbi Judah, a fourth-generation *Tanna* and student of Rabbi Akiba, one of the principals in the tale. The readers of this mishnah would probably also have been aware of this background material and its implications as to the importance of personality in the determination of prayer practices.

The evening prayer is the only *Tefillah* about which Rabbi Judah does not express an opinion. This *Tefillah* has no fixed limit because, as we will see, it is not even mandatory that it be said. This basic controversy over the origins of the *Tefillah* is also addressed in our next *sugya*:

GEMARA (26b): It has been stated: Rabbi Jose son of Rabbi Hanina said, "The *Tefillot* were instituted by the Patriarchs. Rabbi Joshua ben Levi said, "The *Tefillot* were instituted in place of the daily sacrifices. It has likewise been taught in accordance with Rabbi Jose son of Rabbi Hanina, and it has been taught in accordance with Rabbi Joshua ben Levi. It has been taught in accordance with Rabbi Jose, son of Rabbi Hanina: Abraham instituted the morning *Tefillah*, as it is said, "And Abraham arose early in the morning to the place where he had stood" (Genesis 19:27) and "standing" [the Hebrew root *ayin-mem-dalet*] means only in prayer, as it says, "Then Phineas stood up and prayed" (Psalms 106:30).

Isaac instituted the afternoon *Tefillah*, as it is said, "And Isaac went out to meditate in the field at eventide" (Genesis 24:63), and "meditation" [the Hebrew root *sin-yud-chet*] means only prayer, as it says, "A prayer of the afflicted when he faints and pours out his meditation before the Lord" (Psalms 102:1).

Jacob instituted the evening prayer, as it says, "And he lighted [the Hebrew root *pey-gimel-ayin*] upon the place" (Genesis 28:11) and *pegiah* means only prayer, as it says, "Therefore, pray not for this people neither lift up prayer nor cry for them, neither make intercession [*tifga*] to Me" (Jeremiah 7:16).

It has been taught also in accordance with Rabbi Joshua ben Levi: Why did they say that the morning *Tefillah* could be said till midday? Because the regular morning sacrifice could be brought up to midday. Rabbi Judah says [that it may be said] up to the fourth hour because the regular morning sacrifice was brought up to the fourth hour.

And why did they say that the afternoon *Tefillah* can be said up to the evening? Because the regular afternoon offering can be brought up to the evening. Rabbi Judah says [that it can be said] only up to the middle of the afternoon, because the evening offering could only be brought up to the middle of the afternoon.

And why did they say that for the evening *Tefillah* there is no limit? Because the limbs and the fat which were not consumed [on the altar] by the evening could be brought for the whole of the night.

And why did they say that the additional *Tefillahs* could be said during the whole of the day? Because the additional offering could be brought during the whole of the day. Rabbi Judah says [that it can be said only] up to the seventh hour, because the additional offering can be brought up to the seventh hour. . . .

Rabbi Jose son of Rabbi Hanina can answer, "I can still maintain that the Patriarchs instituted the *Tefillot*, and the Rabbis found a basis for them in the sacrifices. For if you do not assume this, who, according to Rabbi Jose son of Rabbi Hanina, instituted the Additional Prayer? He must hold therefore that the Patriarchs instituted the *Tefillahs* and the Rabbis found a basis for them in the offerings."

Why was there a dispute regarding the origins of the *Tefillah*? If the *Tefillot* did not stem from the sacrificial cult, what was their origin? The rabbis found a basis for the *Tefillot* in the Torah. First of all, this undid the link between the *Tefillot* and the Temple, a desirable outcome since there seemed little hope of reestablishing the Temple cult in the immediate future. They wanted to make the *Tefillot* independent of the eventual restoration of the Temple cult. The rabbis may have felt uncomfortable reminding Jews of this national calamity—their inability to rebuild the Temple—three times a day, and preferred to find a basis for them in Scriptures. Such a basis would have emphasized the importance of the *Amidah* by highlighting its ancient, and holy, roots.

However, it seems clear that the *Tefillot* were established to correspond to the sacrifices. This is especially clear when we consider the *Musaf Tefillot*, the additional *Tefillot* said on Shabbat and holidays, which correspond to the additional sacrifices that were brought on those days. There could be no other reason to recite them other than that they correspond to the sacrifices.

The rabbis end up compromising in their characteristic fashion: including both opinions rather than adopting only one. They concede that the rabbis found a basis for the *Tefillot* in the sacrifices, but they state that their true origin extends back to the time of the patriarchs. Perhaps the following analogy will help explain. Imagine that the countdown to midnight on New Year's eve and the "big apple" dropping at Times Square were very, very important to you. Now imagine that New York was conquered by an invading army. The first New Year's eve after the invasion, at precisely 10 seconds before midnight, you counted down and then lit a candle to remind you of the great festivity that used to take place in New York. This situation continues for years, and so you explain your ritual and its antecedents to your child. She has never seen the big apple drop at Times Square, but she knows how important it was to you, and the candle lighting is meaningful to her, so she adopts your practice each New Year's eve. Now imagine that this situation lasts for some 200 years. Your great-great-grandchildren love the ritual, but they understand only vaguely how it started. So they make up new stories to explain to their children why they count down to New Year's eve and light a candle. They always include something about Times Square in the explanation (that much has been passed on), but they embellish the story and tell their children that this was a family tradition that began when their ancestors came to America on a boat from Europe. Over time the ritual has lost its patriotic connotation and become a family tradition. (After all, what was an invading army to you has been the status quo for many years by the time your great-great-grandchildren are born.) That process is something like what is going on here as the rabbis try to explain the origins of the *Tefillah*.

A word about the *drashot* used to link the patriarchs to the *Tefillot*: they are only hinted at in the text, a *remez*. Standing does not always mean prayer. In fact, in the instance with Abraham quoted in the *sugya*, he is standing looking at the destruction God has wrought on Sodom and Gomorrah, not praying. However, this verse links Abraham, the verb *ayin-mem-dalet*, and the morning, so it was used by the rabbis. Similarly, the verse with Isaac links him to a verb that could relate to prayer at a time near sunset. The verse about Jacob links him to a verb that could mean "to pray" during the evening hours. However, the rabbis are using meanings only hinted at in the text to find a link between the *Tefillot* and the patriarchs. A reading of the plain meaning of the Torah text would give us no explicit proof that the patriarchs developed the various *Tefillot*. This doesn't mean that they didn't establish them: it just means there is no straightforward written record of their having done so.

If the patriarchs had in fact developed all three *Tefillot*, then there would not have been a controversy over the obligatory nature of the evening *Tefillah*. This evening *Amidah* was considered optional until Rabban Gamaliel tried to make it compulsory after the Temple was destroyed. This attempt to transform the evening *Amidah* into an obligatory prayer involved a tremendous power struggle. As you read the following story, bear in mind that Rabban Gamaliel was struggling to establish a uniform Jewish practice that could survive the destruction of the Temple, the dispersion of the Jewish population, and the wrecking of the Jewish state, and to unify the Jewish people amidst all these troubles. At such a time of crisis, he exercised his authority quite firmly in order to stabilize the situation and centralize control over Jewish religious life.

GEMARA (27b): Our Rabbis taught: It is told that one student came before Rabbi Joshua and said to him, "Is the evening *Tefillah* optional or obligatory?" He replied, "It is optional."

He then went before Rabban Gamaliel and said to him, "Is the evening *Tefillah* optional or obligatory?" He replied, "It is obligatory." He said to him [Rabban Gamaliel], "Did not Rabbi Joshua tell me that it is optional?" He said, "Wait till the champions enter the Beit HaMidrash."

When the champions came in, the questioner stood and asked, "Is the evening *Tefillah* optional or obligatory?" Rabban Gamaliel replied, "It is obligatory." Said Rabban Gamaliel to the Sages, "Is there anyone who disputes this?" Rabbi Joshua said to him, "No." He said to him [Joshua], "Did they not report you to me as saying that it is optional?"

He said to him, "Joshua, stand up and let them testify against you!" Rabbi Joshua stood up and said, "Were I alive and he [the witness] dead, the living could contradict the dead. But now that he is alive and I am alive, how can the living contradict the living?"

Rabban Gamaliel remained sitting and expounding and Rabbi Joshua remained standing, until the whole crowd began shouting and said to Huzpit the announcer, "Stop!" And he stopped. They then said, "How long is he [Rabban Gamaliel] to go on insulting him [Rabbi Joshua]? On New Year last year he insulted him; he insulted him in the matter of the firstborn in the affair of Rabbi Zadok; now he insults him again! Come, let us depose him!

"Whom shall we appoint instead? Can we appoint Rabbi Joshua? [No] Because he is one of the parties involved. Can we appoint Rabbi Akiba? [No] Because perhaps Rabban Gamaliel will bring a curse on him because he has no ancestral merit. Rather, let us appoint Rabbi Eleazar ben Azariah, for he is wise and he is rich and he is the tenth in descent from Ezra. He is wise, so that if anyone puts a question to him he will be able to answer it. He is rich, so that if occasion arises for paying court to Caesar he will be able to do so. He is tenth in descent from Ezra, so that he has ancestral merit and he [Rabban Gamaliel] cannot bring a curse on him."

They went and said to him, "Will Your Honor consent to become head of the Academy?" He said to them, "I will go and consult the members of my family." He went and consulted his wife. She said to him (28a), "Perhaps they will depose you [later on]?" He said to her, "[There is a proverb:] Let a man use a cup of honor for one day even if it be broken the next." She said to him, "You have no white hair." He was eighteen years old that day, and a miracle was wrought for him and eighteen rows of his hair turned white. That is why Rabbi Eleazar ben Azariah said, "Behold I am *about* seventy years old," and he did not say [simply] seventy years old. [See the end of Chapter 1 for more on this quote.]

A Tanna taught: On that day the doorkeeper was removed and permission was given to the students to enter. For Rabban Gamaliel had issued a proclamation saying, "No student whose character does not correspond to his exterior may enter the *Beit HaMidrash*." On that day many stools were added. Rabbi Johanan said, "There is a difference of opinion on this matter between Abba Joseph ben Dosethai and the Rabbis: one [authority] said that four hundred stools were added, and the other said seven hundred. Rabban Gamaliel became alarmed and said, "Perhaps, God forbid, I withheld Torah from Israel!" He was shown in his dream white casks full of ashes. This, however, really meant nothing: he was only shown this to set his mind at rest.

A Tanna taught: *Eduyot* was formulated on that day, and wherever the expression "on that day" is used, it refers to that day. And there was no halacha pending in the *Beit HaMidrash* which was not expounded. And Rabban Gamaliel did not absent himself from the *Beit HaMidrash* for even a single hour, as we have learnt: On that day Judah, an Ammonite proselyte, came before them in the *Beit HaMidrash*. He said to them, "Am I permitted to enter the assembly?" Said Rabban Gamaliel to him, "You are forbidden to enter the Assembly." Rabbi Joshua said to him, "You are permitted to enter the assembly." Has it not already been said, "An Ammonite or a Moabite shall not enter into the assembly of the Lord" (Deuteronomy 23:4)? Rabbi Joshua replied to him, "Do Ammon and Moab still reside in their original homes? Sennacherib, King of Assyria, long ago went up and mixed up all the nations, as it is said, 'I have removed the bounds of the peoples, and have robbed their treasures, and have brought down, as one mighty, their inhabitants' (Isaiah 10:13) and whatever is separated [from a group] is assumed to belong to the larger section of the group. Said Rabban Gamaliel to him, "But has it not been said, 'But afterward I will bring back the captivity of the children of Ammon, saith the

Lord' (Jeremiah 49:6) so that they have already returned?" Rabbi
Joshua said to him, "And has it not already been said, 'And I
will turn the captivity of my people Israel' (Amos 9:14) and they
have not yet returned?" They immediately permitted him to enter the congregation.

Rabban Gamaliel said, "This being the case, I will go and
apologize to Rabbi Joshua." When he reached his house he saw
that the walls were black. He said to him, "From the walls of
your house it is apparent that you are a charcoal-burner." He
replied, "Alas for the generation of which you are the leader
seeing that you know nothing of the troubles of the scholars,
how they struggle to support and sustain themselves!" He said
to him, "I apologize, forgive me." He paid no attention to him.
"Do it for my father's honor!" He was appeased.

They said, "Who will go and tell the Rabbis?" A certain fuller
said to them, "I will go." Rabbi Joshua sent [a message] to the
Beit HaMidrash saying, "Let him who is accustomed to wear the
robe wear it. Shall he who is not accustomed to wear the robe
say to him who is accustomed to wear it, 'Send me your robe
and I will wear it?'"

Rabbi Akiba said to the Rabbis, "Lock the doors so that the
slaves of Rabban Gamaliel should not come and upset the Rabbis." Said Rabbi Joshua, "I had better get up and go to them
myself." He came and knocked at the door. He said to them,
"Let the sprinkler son of a sprinkler sprinkle [i.e. the priest, the
son of a priest, sprinkle the water of purification]. Shall he who
is neither a sprinkler nor the son of a sprinkler say to a sprinkler
son of a sprinkler, 'Your water is cave water and your ashes are
oven ashes?'" Rabbi Akiba said to him, "Rabbi Joshua, are you
appeased? We have done nothing except for the sake of your
honor. Tomorrow you and I will go to his house first thing in the
morning [to make amends]." They said, "[But] how shall we do
it? Shall we depose him [Rabbi Eleazar ben Azariah]? We have a
tradition that one may raise an object to a higher degree of holiness but one must not degrade it to a lower one." Let one Master
preach on one Sabbath and one on the next. [No, because] this
will cause jealousy. Rather, let Rabban Gamaliel preach three
Sabbaths and Rabbi Eleazar ben Azariah one Sabbath...And
that student [who asked the original question] was Rabbi Shimon ben Yochai.

This story seems to be the ultimate expression of the inter-action of prayer and personality. Clearly we are dealing with far more than whether the evening *Tefillah* is compulsory or optional. We are also examining how conflicts are managed, how important the maintenance of relationships is in Judaism, and what kind of personality is most desirable in a leader of the Jewish people. What kinds of personalities are displayed in this story? There is the autocratic personality of Rabban Gamaliel II. He succeeded Yochanan ben Zachai as president of the Academy in Yavneh around 80 C.E. His life's goal was to strengthen both Yavneh as the center of Jewish life after Jerusalem was conquered and the position of the Nasi (president of the Academy). He was so autocratic that he was opposed by the other sages.

Rabbi Joshua ben Chananiah, on the other hand, was a peace-loving soul. Generally, he followed the rulings of Beit Hillel. For instance, he was liberal in admitting proselytes, as we see from this story. He was also a Levite, which meant that he came from an aristocratic family. (A modern equivalent would be to belong to the Kennedy or Rockefeller clan.) A certain status went along with membership in a priestly family. Such membership obviously still held some cachet even after the Temple was destroyed. Rabbi Joshua actually served in the Temple as a chorister (*Arakhin* 11b).

The social standing of both Rabban Gamaliel and Rabbi Joshua may have added to the charged atmosphere surround-ing this issue of the evening *Tefillah*. At that point in time the old aristocracy, the priesthood, was giving way to a new one, the aristocracy of the Academy. Rabban Gamaliel may have been publicly trying to make this change explicit and consoli-date power for his position. Rabbi Joshua's opinion that the evening *Tefillah* is optional relates the *Tefillot* to the Temple sacri-fices. Since there was no evening sacrifice, Rabbi Joshua felt the corresponding *Tefillah* was not mandatory. Rabban Gamaliel did not want to relate the *Tefillot* to the cult: he wanted Jewish practice to be determined by the scholars, not the priests. Therefore, he rules that the evening *Tefillah* is obligatory.

Rabban Gamaliel may also have been subtly asserting the authority of *Tannaim* with Babylonian lineages. Rabban Gamaliel's great-great-grandfather was Hillel, a Babylonian. Rabbi Joshua ben Chanania was apparently of purely Palestinian origin. Palestinian sages were the only ones who were ordained, and later, greater authority was ascribed to them than to Babylonian sages. Here, Rabban Gamaliel seems to be subtly evening the score. Something akin to this emotional dimension can be seen in the United States even today. When descendants of Russian-Jewish immigrants take positions of leadership that were formerly reserved for descendants of German-Jewish immigrants, they sometimes do so with a particular relish, as if to say, "Look how far our group has come!" However, old loyalties die hard, and Rabbi Joshua obviously had his supporters.

Rabbi Eleazar ben Azariah was wise, rich, and came from the very best of families. Ezra was a priest *and* a scribe. He was the first forerunner of the Pharisees, who in turn preceded the *Tannaim*. (In American terms, it would be equivalent to being a tenth-generation descendant of George Washington.) Thus Rabbi Eleazar ben Azariah's family maintained an ancient tradition of learning *and* connection to the priesthood. This made him the perfect "compromise individual" for this situation: his elevation to *Nasi* meant recognizing the interests of the priestly families *and* adhering to the study of the Torah as his true base of power.

What requirements did the *Tannaim* deem necessary for a leader of the Jewish people? Like Eleazar ben Azariah, he should be wise, rich, and from a good family. Notice that age is not a determinant. In addition, he should not be autocratic, as was Gamaliel, but rather, he should be able to draw people together. In the end, it is this personality type that prevails. Rabbi Joshua's view was adopted as the *halachah* over Rabban Gamaliel's: the evening *Tefillah* is optional.

Before the story even begins, we learn that Rabban Gamaliel has twice before insulted Rabbi Joshua. On one occasion, he and Rabbi Joshua disagreed about the determination of the Jewish calendar. To demonstrate his authority, Rabban Gamaliel made Rabbi Joshua appear in the *Beit HaMidrash* carrying his staff and his wallet on the day that Rabbi Joshua had determined was Yom Kippur, when such activities are strictly forbidden. Rabban Gamaliel had his reasons, of course. The Jewish people and religion would have disintegrated without a single calendar to follow. Just imagine the confusion that would result if different groups observed Labor Day on different dates, and the problem will quickly become clear.

The other instance, reported in tractate *Bechorot* 36a, bears a striking similarity to our present story. In this case, too, Rabban Gamaliel shames Rabbi Joshua in the Academy. The case in *Bechorot* also touches on the subtle conflict between the scholarly and priestly classes. It involves the consecration of the first-born of animals and people to God. Deuteronomy 15:19–23 outlines this law, including the stipulation that the first-born must have no blemish on it. If there is a blemish on it, the animal may be eaten by the priest rather than sacrificed. The rabbis determined that the priest could eat the beast only if the blemish came about naturally or by accident. However, if the blemish was inflicted intentionally so that the priest might eat the beast or sell it, then it may be neither sacrificed nor eaten nor sold. A nonpriestly Jew would never be able to keep his or her first-born animals, so it made no difference who received it, the Temple cult or a priest. However, priests might be tempted to inflict injuries on their animals so that they could eat them or sell them instead of sacrificing them to the Temple cult. Therefore, Rabban Gamaliel ruled that we do not accept the testimony of a priest regarding the origin of a blemish on a first-born animal, even if that priest is a *chaver*, a person deeply committed to observing the *mitzvot*. Rabbi Zadok was such a priest, and one of his first-born animals accidentally cut its lip. Rabbi Joshua accepted Rabbi Zadok's testimony, allowing him to eat or sell the beast, while Rabban Gamaliel forbade it. Rabban Gamaliel confronted Rabbi Joshua and shamed him in front of the academy, just as he did in the foregoing *sugya*.

A question about the evening *Tefillah* sets the story in motion. Rabban Gamaliel and Rabbi Joshua disagree, and Gamaliel forces the issue in public. Rabbi Joshua attempts to avoid the conflict, but Rabban Gamaliel presses him until he must stand up for his point of view. After Rabban Gamaliel has dispensed with Rabbi Joshua, he lets Joshua continue to stand, publicly shamed. At this, the people in the Academy erupt. They call on Chuzpit, the announcer, to stop. In the Academy,

Rabban Gamaliel would speak in low tones, and Chuzpit would then amplify his message and transmit it to those present. Rabban Gamaliel, who denied students access to the *Beit HaMidrash* because they did not live up to his letter of the law, publicly shames another scholar, which is as serious as killing someone in the Jewish tradition. In Judaism, one's words and one's deeds cannot be separated: we must live what we speak. Rabban Gamaliel did not live up to that ideal, and he therefore lost his power.

The rabbis then ask Rabbi Eleazar ben Azariah to become the *nasi* and he, in turn, consults his wife before giving an answer: *this* is true wisdom! This story moves toward ever greater disintegration of relationships until this moment, the turning point, when God miraculously intervenes. And the intervention is subtle: supplying Rabbi Eleazar ben Azariah with eighteen rows of white hair. This is one of the hidden messages of this story: God's hand may be felt in history, and in our own lives, through small miracles as well as large ones. Now all the conflicts created in the first part of the story will be resolved.

First, the students who had been barred from the *Beit HaMidrash* were allowed back in. The tractate *Eduyot*, "Testimonies," unlike the other tractates of the Mishnah, is a collection of *mishnayot* on a wide variety of topics. This tractate, as we have it now, could not possibly have been taught in its entirety on that day in Yavneh (about 90 C.E.) because it cites many rabbis who lived long after that time. However, a shorter form of this tractate might have been composed on that day. This makes intuitive sense: all the scholarly insights on so many topics had been held in check for so long that, given the opportunity, they rushed out. It may have been an outpouring of intellectual and spiritual enlightenment that, unlike the other tractates of the Mishnah, did not need to be organized according to topic. Rabban Gamaliel feels remorse and fear when he sees how many students he prevented from entering the Academy. He interprets his dream to confirm that he had been right: the students he had barred from the Academy were worthless, like ashes. However, the Gemara confirms that Rabban Gamaliel was wrong: these students were worthy of admission. Rabban Gamaliel seems to be avoiding a true change of heart.

However, he finally does *teshuvah* (i.e., repents) when he accepts Rabbi Joshua's ability to determine the law. The specific case they are debating is the admission of a proselyte from the territory of Ammon. Ammonites and Moabites were prohibited from joining the Jewish people in Deuteronomy 23:4. However, Rabbi Joshua contends that those living in the territory that was Ammon are not the descendants of the Ammonites referred to in the Torah. All the people of the area had been mingled together by Sennacherib of Assyria. And since the majority of people in the area are permitted to convert to Judaism, they accepted this person as well. By "fencing" with these texts from Scripture, Rabbi Joshua outwits Rabban Gamaliel and ensures that the proselyte will be admitted into the Jewish people. By accepting Rabbi Joshua's words, Rabban Gamaliel is swallowing his pride and learning humility. (It is ironic that Rabban Gamaliel's great-great-grandfather, Hillel, was once barred by doormen from entering the Academy and was also liberal in accepting proselytes to Judaism.)

Rabbi Joshua shows his humanity when Rabban Gamaliel apologizes to him. If he were very righteous, he would have accepted Rabban Gamaliel's apology immediately. Instead, he makes Gamaliel apologize twice before accepting his plea. In addition, he takes the opportunity to make Rabban Gamaliel more sensitive. Coming from an aristocratic, very wealthy family, Rabban Gamaliel seemed to have no idea how hard some of the rabbis had to work to maintain themselves. In other words, a leader must understand the lives of his or her people. (For a fascinating discussion of charcoal and the professions related to it, see the El Am Talmud [1982, pp. 576–577]).

Once he has accepted the apology, Rabbi Joshua continues the healing process. Now that he is confident that Rabban Gamaliel has become more sensitive to the conditions under which the other rabbis labor, and now that he is sure that Rabban Gamaliel is more open to other interpretations of the law, he helps Rabban Gamaliel regain his position. Rabbi Joshua seems to acknowledge, by the riddles that he poses to the Academy, that there is room in the Academy for both teachers of priestly origin, like himself, and teachers of scholarly lineage, such as Rabban Gamaliel. The robe to which he refers is the robe of the *nasi*, president of the Academy, which Gamaliel wore by right of being one of Hillel's descendants. The "sprinkler" refers to a priest who combines the ashes of the red heifer and "living water" (water collected from a stream and fit to drink) to perform a purification ceremony (Numbers 19:1–13).

This mention of ashes by Rabbi Joshua may relate to the ashes in Rabban Gamaliel's dream. In both cases, ashes that actually represent something of value (worthy students in Rabban Gamaliel's dream and the efficacy of the priestly cult in Rabbi Joshua's speech) are accused of being worthless (Rabban Gamaliel believes that the ashes mean the students weren't worthy; Rabbi Joshua's ashes are accused of being oven ashes). Again, this symbolism emphasizes the underlying tension between the aristocracy of the Academy and that of the priesthood. In the case of Rabban Gamaliel's dream, he does not perceive the truth: that the students were worthy. But he seems to have finally grasped the worth of the priestly group within the Academy. Certainly the members of the Academy do. They do not readmit Rabban Gamaliel just because, as Rabbi Joshua reminds them with the riddle about the cloak, he has the hereditary right to be the president. They readmit him only when, with his second riddle, Rabbi Joshua implies that *both* priests and scholars belong in the *Beit HaMidrash* and will be accepted.

Perhaps it is just that Rabban Gamaliel is locked out of the *Beit HaMidrash* because his deeds did not match his words, for he did the same to many disciples. Rabban Gamaliel is finally restored to his position, but what of Eliezer ben Azariah? Need he suffer because of this change of events? No, he maintains his elevated status, even though Rabban Gamaliel is made his superior.

Thus, all the relationships are brought into harmony. Rabban Gamaliel is reinstated after he repents. Rabbi Joshua is appeased. The value of both the scholarly and the priestly lineages is recognized. The students are readmitted to the *Beit HaMidrash*. The proselyte is accepted as a Jew, and Rabbi Eleazar ben Azariah is allowed to maintain his elevated status.

This story has many important messages for us today. Who ought to hold power in the modern Jewish community?

Those whose deeds match their words. *These* are the leaders we should follow. Those who are able to maintain relationships, who accept apologies, who do not exclude people from learning, and most important, who live what they teach are the true leaders of our people, whatever their institutional affiliations.

Rabban Gamaliel and Rabbi Joshua disagreed about other issues related to the *Amidah* besides the evening *Tefillah*.

MISHNAH (28b): Rabban Gamaliel says, "Everyday a person should pray the Eighteen Benedictions." Rabbi Joshua says, "An abbreviated [form of the] Eighteen Benedictions." Rabbi Akiba says, "If he knows the *Tefillah* fluently he prays the [full] Eighteen Benedictions, and if not, [let him pray] an abbreviated [form of the] Eighteen Benedictions." Rabbi Eliezer says, "If a man makes his prayers a fixed task it is not a [genuine] supplication."

Rabbi Joshua says, "One who is walking in a dangerous place, prays a short *Tefillah*, and says, 'Save, O Lord, Your people, the remnant of Israel. In every time of crisis may their needs be before You. Blessed are You, O Lord, who hearkens to prayer.'"

If one was riding on an ass, one dismounts and prays. If one is unable to dismount, one should turn one's face [towards Jerusalem]; and if one cannot turn one's face one should concentrate one's thoughts on the Holy of Holies. If one is traveling on a ship or a raft, one should concentrate one's thoughts on the Holy of Holies."

GEMARA: To what do these Eighteen Benedictions correspond? Rabbi Hillel the son of Rabbi Samuel bar Nahmani said, "To the eighteen times that David mentioned the Divine Name in the psalm [which begins], 'Ascribe unto the Lord, O ye sons of might'" (Psalm 29). Rav Joseph said, "To the eighteen times the Divine Name is mentioned in the Recitation of the Shema." Rabbi Tanhum said in the name of Rabbi Joshua ben Levi, "To the eighteen vertebrae in the spinal column." . . .

These eighteen are really nineteen? Rabbi Levi said, "The benediction relating to the Minim was instituted in Yavneh. To what was it meant to correspond?" Rabbi Levi said, "According to Rabbi Hillel the son of Rabbi Samuel bar Nahmani, to 'the God of Glory thunders' (Psalm 29:3) [counting this as another mention of God's name in that same psalm]." According to

Rabbi Joseph, to the word 'One' in the Shema [counting it as another mention of one of God's names]. On the view of Rabbi Tanhum quoting Rabbi Joshua ben Levi, to the little vertebrae in the spinal column.

In this encounter between Rabban Gamaliel and Rabbi Joshua, Rabbi Akiba plays a mediating role. Now, the two great *Tannaim* are discussing what exactly constitutes a valid recitation of the *Tefillah*. Gamaliel mandates that the full eighteen benedictions be said. Joshua, maintaining his liberal bent, allows an abbreviated form of the *Tefillah*. This abbreviated form consists of the first three blessings, a short middle section in which each intermediate blessing is reduced to one phrase or sentence, and the last three blessings. (The actual prayer follows.)

Both Rabbi Eliezer and Rabbi Joshua emphasize that it is an individual's *inner* state during prayer that is crucial to the prayer's being properly said. The individual must express the genuine feelings of the heart. Rabbi Joshua recognizes that when one is in danger, one will not have the ability to luxuriate in prayer and petition God for the various blessings found in the *Tefillah*. Better to delay the *Tefillah* until it can be said with true intention.

The sages also show flexibility when prescribing one's physical posture during the *Amidah*. Ideally, one should stand facing, respectively, Israel, Jerusalem, and the Holy of Holies. This set of priorities governs synagogue architecture to this day in both the United States and Israel. However, if we have no way of knowing in which direction to turn, or if we are not able to turn in the prescribed direction, we use our mental powers to overcome our physical situation, just as we did when dealing with the *tefillin* in the privy. The mind has the power to shape reality.

"Why exactly eighteen benedictions?" the rabbis ask. The answers are not as fanciful as they first appear. Eighteen, of course, stands for *chai*, "life," in numerology. But this is too abstract a basis on which to found such a deeply felt prayer. The prayer is based on our intellect (verses from Torah, which we appreciate with our minds), our souls (which correspond to the God we affirm in the *Shema*, as we just saw), and our bodies (which are held together by the spine). In addition, the Yerushalmi relates the eighteen benedictions to the eighteen times "Abraham, Isaac, and Jacob" are mentioned in the Torah. And whether there are eighteen or nineteen benedictions, which is the number of benedictions we say today, the bases for the prayer are the same: mind, soul, body, and tradition.

The law follows Rabbi Akiba in the matter of the shortened *Amidah*. We may say a shortened *Tefillah* only when time is quite short (that is, we are saying the *minchah* [the afternoon] *Tefillah*, and we are running out of time, as the sun is about to set) or when we are in danger. Of course, the rabbis want to determine exactly what form the shortened *Tefillah* will take.

> **GEMARA (29a):** "Rabbi Joshua says, 'An abbreviated Eighteen [Benedictions].'" What is an abbreviated [form of the] Eighteen [Benedictions]? Rav said, "An abbreviated form of each blessing." And Samuel said, "Give us discernment, O Lord, to know Your ways, and circumcise our heart to fear You, and forgive us so that we may be redeemed, and keep us far from our sufferings, and fatten us in the pastures of Your land, and gather our scattered ones from the four corners of the earth, and let them who go astray be judged according to Your will, and raise Your hand against the wicked, and let the righteous rejoice in the building of Your city and the establishment of Your Temple, and in the exalting of the horn of David Your servant and the preparation of a light for the son of Jesse Your Messiah. Before we call may You answer; blessed are You, O Lord, who hearkens to prayer."

This abbreviated form of the intermediate blessings is called *Havineinu*, "grant us," after the first word of this prayer. It can be found in prayer books to this day. It may be said every day except Saturday nights, the nights after holidays end, and the days between the end of Sukkot and the beginning of Pesach. On each of these occasions, we add special prayers to the *Tefillah* (*Havdalah* on Saturday nights and the nights after holidays, and requests for rain during the winter), and so we must say the full *Tefillah* in order to insert the special prayers.

The phrases if the *Havineinu* correspond to the blessings of the middle section of the *Tefillah* as follows:

Understanding: "Give us discernment, O Lord, to know Thy ways,

Repentance: and circumcise our heart to fear You, and forgive us

Forgiveness: so that we may be redeemed,

Healing: and keep us far from our sufferings,

The Blessing of the Year: and fatten us in the pastures of Your land,

Ingathering of the Exiles: and gather our dispersions from the four corners of the earth

Justice: and let them who err from Your prescriptions be punished,

Minim: and lift up Your hand against the wicked,

Tsadikim: and let the righteous rejoice

Jerusalem: in the building of Your city and the establishment of the temple

Messiah Son of David: and in the exalting of the horn of David Your servant and the preparation of a light for the son of Jesse Your Messiah;

Supplication: before we call may You answer; blessed are You, O Lord, who hearkens to prayer."

The *halachah* legislates flexibility in prayer. We are to make the *Tefillah* the true expression of our hearts and souls: our own individual interaction of prayer and personality. The recital of the *Shema* is not as flexible because it is not intended as a vehicle for personal expression. The *Tefillah*, however, is each individual's prayer, and the rabbis affirm that each of us is allowed, even encouraged, to find our own route to God through the different forms of the *Tefillah*, as we see in the following comment from the Gemara:

> **GEMARA (29b)**: "Rabbi Eliezer says, 'He who makes his prayer a fixed task . . .'" What is meant by a "fixed task"? Rabbi Jacob bar Idi said in the name of Rabbi Oshaiah, "Anyone whose prayer is like a burden on him." The Rabbis say, "Whoever does not say it in the manner of supplications." Rabba and Rav Joseph both say, "Whoever cannot say something new in it."

Contrary to some characterizations of traditional Judaism, spontaneity in worship is encouraged. Rabbi Jacob bar Idi requires an even higher level of intention than do the majority of sages. He feels that each time a person says the *Tefillah*, it must be said with deep feelings of need and love. The sages allow a person to say the *Tefillah* merely as a supplication.

These different approaches can be likened to a couple who sits down to negotiate a solution to a problem. It sometimes seems easier to have this kind of conversation without revealing one's emotions, to get the problem out on the table, solve it, and not deal with the feelings that go along with it. But that kind of conversation, while useful, does not help build a relationship. As a matter of fact, such conversations may stifle true intimacy if that is all the relationship consists of. True, the relationship will function, but not on the level of feelings. The sages maintain that it is enough for our relationship with God to function, but the *ideal* is for it to be a full-bodied relationship of true intimacy.

The *Tefillah* may be abbreviated to a form even shorter than the *Havineinu* if some danger is lurking at the time we are to recite it.

> **GEMARA (29b)**: Our Rabbis taught, "One who is walking in a place infested with beasts or robbers prays a short *Tefillah*." What is a short *Tefillah*?
>
> Rabbi Eliezer says, "Do Your will in heaven above, and give relief to the spirit of them that fear You below, and do what is good in Your eyes. Blessed are You, O Lord, who hearkens to prayer."
>
> Rabbi Joshua says, "Hear the supplication of Your people Israel and speedily fulfill their plea. Blessed are You, O Lord, who hearkens to prayer."

Rabbi Eleazar son of Rabbi Zadok says, "Hear the cry of Your people Israel and speedily fulfill their request. Blessed are You, O Lord, who hearkens to prayer."

Others say, "The needs of Your people Israel are many and their wit is small. May it be Your will, O Lord our God, to give to each one enough for his sustenance and to each body enough for its needs. Blessed are You, O Lord, who hearkens to prayer."

Rav Huna said, "The *halachah* follows the 'Others'" . . .

GEMARA (30a): What is the difference between "Havineinu" and the Short Prayer? "Havineinu" requires the recital of the first and last three [blessings of the *Amidah*], and when he returns home he need not say the *Tefillah* again. The Short Prayer does not require the recital of either by the first or the last three [blessings of the *Amidah*], and when one returns home he must say the *Tefillah*.

The rabbis continue to examine the conditions under which one might say a modified version of the *Tefillah*. Unlike our preceding *sugya*, which outlined choices for us in situations of calm and quiet, we now posit that we are in danger. In a dangerous situation, we are to say this very short *Tefillah* without the first three and last three blessings. We wouldn't be in the frame of mind, or even able, perhaps, to approach God, make a petition, and then thank God. All we would be able to say sincerely is "Help!" Once the danger has passed, we go back and say the whole *Tefillah*.

This can be likened to two different situations with a child. In one, he sidles up to his parent, flatters the parent, asks for a treat, and then shows effusive thanks to the parent. In the other, when he is in danger, he yells, with great sincerity, for help; there is no approach, no flattery, and no thanks—just a relieved embrace once the danger is over.

The different prayers reflect the personalities of the rabbis who composed them. Rabbi Eliezer's prayer seems to fit his strict character: it is an unconditional submission to God's will. Perhaps that is why it was not chosen as the prayer we say when endangered: most people could not sincerely say this prayer in such a circumstance.

Rabbi Joshua's prayer, on the other hand, poses a different problem. He asks God to fulfill our requests, but our requests might not be for our benefit. For example, if your car broke down on a country road at night, you might pray that the next car that came by would stop for you. But what if that car was full of robbers? It would be better for you if God did *not* grant your prayer in this case. Rabbi Eleazar b. Zadok's prayer is identical to Rabbi Joshua's except for one word: he asks that our *cries* be heard rather than our supplications.

The prayer that is accepted for general use is the last one, attributed to the anonymous majority. This prayer acknowledges that we may not know exactly what to pray for in a dangerous situation. It calls on God to use God's own judgment.

In this chapter, the rabbis outlined the ways in which we can express our personal, political, physical, and emotional needs in prayer. Who we are affects our relationship with God, and vice versa. Optimally, the relationship is a mutually elevating one.

5

Piety and Apostasy

W hat happens when our personalities have an intense impact on our spiritual lives, and vice versa? What happens when we either move in the direction of extreme devotion to God or violently break away from God? That is the question addressed in this chapter. Having explored the intersection of personality and prayer in Chapter 4, the rabbis now examine this concept in a more intense form in Chapter 5. This chapter, the second, and last, which deals with the *Amidah*, explores the concepts of piety and apostasy. This theme flows naturally from the discussion in Chapter 4 of prayer and personality. We move from that topic to the subject of the interaction of personality and devotion, or the lack thereof, in one's *whole life*, not just during prayer. This theme also forms a thematic bridge to the last half of the tractate, which is concerned with the interaction of the Holy and everyday life, outside of specific, regulated moments of prayer. This chapter closes the first major section of the tractate. It ends with a *nechemtah*, a word of comfort and hope, which summarizes this chapter's theme: the inward nature of piety.

The chapter begins with a mishnah that, like those in Chapter 4, concentrates on the correct recital of the *Amidah*.

MISHNAH (30b): One should not stand up to say the *Tefillah* unless one is in a serious frame of mind. The first Chasidim used to wait an hour before praying in order that they might concentrate their thoughts upon their Father in Heaven. Even if a king

81

greets him [while praying] he should not answer him. Even if a
snake is wound round his heel, he should not break off.

Our mishnah begins by defining the underlying subject of
the chapter: how does piety manifest itself? The mishnah defines piety as *koved rosh*, serious-mindedness. We may define
piety as the degree to which an individual manifests an intense
and fulfilling relationship with the one God in *all* aspects of his
or her life, not just during prayer. Here is the difference between the themes of the last chapter and this one. Chapter 4
dealt with the interaction of personality and prayer. In this
chapter we explore the interaction of personality and the total
relationship with God at all times, not just during prayer (although prayer, as direct communication, plays a large role in
piety).

This mishnah outlines piety in an ascending order of intensity. It begins with the minimum requirement: saying the
Tefillah reverently, then moves up to the level of the *Chasidim
Rishonim*, the first, or early, pious ones. They maintained a
higher standard of observance and morality than was the
norm. They were constantly ready to undergo purification and
offer atonement sacrifices if they were at all suspicious that
they had sinned. And they took great care to maintain their
relationships with humans and with God.

The ideal pious relationship with God requires great concentration and intensity. It is one that brooks no interruption,
even from a king or a serpent. How different this is from the
Shema, whose recital we are permitted to interrupt! This would
seem an apparent contradiction: how can we be permitted to
make a break while reciting the *Shema* but not while reciting the
Tefillah? The *Shema* is a declaration, not a plea for mercy, and so
one might not feel quite as vulnerable during its recitation as
one would feel while reciting the *Amidah*. Consequently, inter-
ruptions would not disturb our concentration as much. The
Amidah, on the other hand, is an expression of need: it has an
individual quality and an urgency that the *Shema* does not. In
general, the more needy we feel, the more potent a prayer the
Amidah will be for us.

A modern-day example of this phenomenon might happen in a bank. Imagine that you go to the bank every day and, while there, greet the manager. If someone interrupts you as you greet her, you will probably not feel distressed. Now imagine that you are seeing the manager in order to borrow some money. The more you need the money, the more nervous you will feel. Anything that interrupts your conversation with the manager will feel uncomfortable at best and devastating at worst. If you were truly desperate, you would be able to concentrate on the manager so intently that you could block out all the distractions around you. The "greeting mode" is analagous to the *Shema*, while the "borrowing mode" is analogous to the *Amidah* and the intensity with which it is said.

When we say the *Amidah*, we say it with great urgency. We may relate to God so intensely that we become oblivious to outside distractions, just as the *Chasidim Rishonim* did. Mar, the son of Ravina, epitomized this sort of concentration.

GEMARA (30b): Mar the son of Ravina made a marriage feast for his son. He saw that the Rabbis were growing very merry (31a), so he brought a precious cup worth four hundred zuz and broke it before them, and they became serious.

Rav Ashi made a marriage feast for his son. He saw that the Rabbis were growing very merry, so he brought a cup of white crystal and broke it before them and they became serious.

The Rabbis said to Rav Hamnuna Zuti at the wedding of Mar the son of Ravina, "Let the Master sing us something."

He said to them, "Alas for us that we shall die! Alas for us that we shall die!"

They said to him, "What shall we respond after you ?"

He said to them, "Where is the Torah and where is the mitzvah that will shield us!"

Here the Gemara shows us that true piety extends to all the moments of our lives; it is not limited to moments of prayer. We must remember at every moment that a spark of the Divine, our souls, resides within us, and act accordingly. So Mar, the son of Ravina, shocks the rabbis into remembering themselves by breaking a glass. (This is one possible interpretation for the shattering of a glass at a wedding: if we forget that part of God resides in us, our lives will be shattered.)

The figure of Mar bar Ravina may seem unsympathetic at first, but we can have some empathy for him once we understand him. He is like many traditional Jews today who seem priggish and straitlaced. It may help if we think of such persons as we would think of a pregnant woman. When a woman is pregnant, her first priority must be to guard the vulnerable, pure being inside her. She might like to drink, but if she is a responsible person, she will forgo alcoholic beverages for the sake of her fetus. She might like to stay out late and go dancing, but she abstains from this behavior, too, if it will harm the baby. And usually she will do so willingly because she is protecting something important by forgoing these pleasures.

A person who has internalized a great deal of Torah is like a pregnant woman. Such a person has a mass of pure "Torahness" inside him or her that, like a fetus, must be nurtured and protected. Thus, for example, some traditional Jews might like to look at pictures of scantily clad models, but they do not do so because they are protecting that pure mass of Torah within themselves. (Of course, this does not give them the license to ban such pictures, just as we do not forbid women who are pregnant to drink alcoholic beverages.) Mar bar Ravina and the other rabbis in this *sugya* who appear so severe are guarding the purity of the Torah that they have so painstakingly internalized. A person with a large mass of Torah inside him or her must guard against even the *appearance* of defiling that mass, just as a pregnant woman ought to forgo giving even the appearance of doing something that would endanger her fetus.

The song sung at Mar bar Ravina's wedding drives home a point about piety: that Torah and *mitzvot*, along with family, are the things that live on after us. Significantly, when we name a baby, we wish it a life of Torah, *chuppah*, and *ma'asim tovim*— Torah, marriage, and children, and good deeds. If we fill our lives with these three things, we will have ensured our own immortality.

This drive to achieve immortality can be seen in the following *sugya* as well:

GEMARA (31a): Our Rabbis taught: One should not stand up to pray *Tefillah* when filled with sorrow, idleness, laughter, idle conversation, chatter, lightheadedness, or idle things, but only while [one is] still rejoicing in the performance of some religious act.

Similarly a person should not take leave of one's friend with ordinary conversation, joking, lightheadedness, idle talk, but with some matter of halachah.

How do we prepare ourselves to say the *Tefillah*? By raising our self-esteem. Ironically, the less needy we feel, the easier it becomes to ask God for things. How do we raise our self-esteem? By engaging in a *mitzvah*, such as reciting the prayer praising God for the exodus from Egypt, reciting a psalm, such as Psalm 144, or seeing to the needs of the community.

The ability of healthy, appropriate self-esteem to facilitate prayer is also seen in the following *sugya*.

GEMARA (34a): Rav Judah said, "A person should never petition for his requirements either in the first three [benedictions of the Amidah] nor in the last three, but in the middle ones." For Rabbi Hanina said, "In the first ones he resembles a servant who is setting forth the praise of his master, in the middle ones he resembles a servant who is requesting a reward from his master, in the last ones he resembles a servant who has received a reward from his master and he takes his leave and goes away." . . .

GEMARA (34a): Our Rabbis taught: These are the benedictions [of the *Tefillah*] in which a person bows: the benediction of the patriarchs, beginning and end, and the [Benediction of] Thanksgiving, beginning and end. If one wants to bow down at the end of each benediction and at the beginning of each benediction, he is instructed not to do so.

Rabbi Simeon ben Pazzi said in the name of Rabbi Joshua ben Levi, reporting Bar Kappara: "An ordinary person bows as we have mentioned (34b); a high priest [bows] at the end of each benediction; a king [bows] at the beginning of each benediction and at the end of each benediction."

One of the aspects of God we encounter most frequently is God's sovereign nature. Certainly the movements we make when saying the *Tefillah* express our dependence on God. We step back in order to then approach God, bowing in respect. When we are finished, we step back, still turned to God, bowing as we take our leave. And the greater our earthly power, the more bowing the rabbis prescribe. They want to reinforce our awareness of God's ultimate power over our lives—a concept that we might resist.

On the other hand, we are not to humble ourselves too much. If one wants to bow at the beginning and end of each prayer, one is not permitted to do so. The rabbis do not want us to have an unhealthy vision of ourselves as totally powerless save for God's help. On the contrary, they want us to take control of our lives and our souls. They urge us to maintain that delicate balance between overconfidence and healthy self-esteem; between low self-esteem and healthy humility.

The rabbis have given us the guidelines that can facilitate piety—an intense, love-filled connection with God. However, piety must rise from the individual's heart; after a certain point, it is not a skill that can be taught. This deep desire to make a connection with God can be likened to any other talent with which we are graced at birth. For example, Mikhail Baryshnikov had wonderful ballet training, but training alone could not make him dance as he does: his talent is something deep within him. Similarly, some people have more of a drive to make a connection with God than do others. Rabbi Akiba was one in whom this drive was very strong. He serves as a role model of a truly pious person.

> **GEMARA (31a):** Such was the custom of Rabbi Akiba: when he would pray with the congregation, he would cut [his prayer] short and rise in order not to inconvenience the congregation. But when he prayed by himself, a person could leave him in one corner and find him [later] in another, on account of his many genuflections and prostrations.

Piety is a private phenomenon, not a public one. If true piety is displayed in public, it is transformed into arrogance and self-righteousness. The truly pious don't need to demonstrate their fervor. It radiates from them and inspires us without their uttering a word.

Akiba is a great exemplar of this principle. He did not want to force his lengthy prayers on the congregation. For him, such prayer was a genuine expression of his soul. For them, it would be a caricature of prayer. Such devotion may also have been so precious that he may not have wanted to offer it up to public scrutiny. Akiba's piety was finally demonstrated publicly when he was executed by the Romans (see Chapter 9).

Apparently some persons had not learned that piety is a private phenomenon. The following *sugya* demonstrates what happens when we try to put private devotion on public display.

GEMARA (33b): A certain [reader] went down in the presence of Rabbi Hanina and said, "God, the great, mighty, awesome, majestic, powerful, awful, strong, fearless, sure and honored." He waited till he had finished. When he had finished he said to him, "Have you finished all the praise of your Master? What do I need all [these adjectives] for? Even with these three that we do say ["great, mighty, and awesome"], had not Moses our Teacher said them in the Torah (Deuteronomy 10:17) and had not the Men of the Great Assembly (Nehemiah 9:32) come and set them in the *Tefillah*, we would not have been able to say them, and you say all these [three] and still go on! It is as if a king of flesh and blood had a million denarii of gold, and someone praised him for some silver ones. Would it not be an insult to him?"

The *shaliach tsibbur*, the person leading the *Tefillah*, in this story was apparently not expressing piety in the correct way. He stood up to pray and, as was the custom, knew the basic outline of the prayers but felt free to vary them. He went on and on, praising God far more than does the standard version of this prayer, the *Avot*. Rabbi Hanina, instead of praising his fervor, rebukes him for his presumptuousness. We are limited in our ability to understand God and thus also in our ability to praise God. To assume that we can adequately praise God is presumptuous.

The rabbis here reveal two sides of an issue. In Chapter 4, we learned that we must be able to add something fresh to our *Tefillah* each time we say it. On the other hand, there are prayers that the rabbis believe we should say exactly as they have been handed down to us. The key is knowing when to be creative: we can add fresh things to our requests, since we know our needs. We must not add to the praise of God (the first three blessings and the last three) because to do so implies that we know every aspect of God and can adequately praise God. Given that our minds and souls are finite, and God is infinite, this can never be. Sometimes the humblest praise is the highest.

Two biblical exemplars of piety are David and Hannah, the mother of the prophet Samuel, whose prayer (1 Samuel 1:1–2:10) we read as the *Haftarah* on the first day of Rosh HaShanah. As Hannah prayed, so are we adjured to pray.

> **GEMARA (31a):** Rav Hamnuna said, "How many important laws can be learnt from these verses relating to Hannah (1 Samuel 1:10ff.)!" "Now Hannah, spoke in her heart": from this we learn that one who prays must direct his heart.
>
> "Only her lips moved": from this we learn that one who prays must frame the words distinctly with his lips.
>
> "But her voice could not be heard": from this, it is forbidden to raise one's voice in the *Tefillah*.
>
> "And Eli thought she had been drunken": from this, that a drunken person is forbidden to say the *Tefillah*.

As they did in Chapter 4, the rabbis are basing the *Amidah* on a biblical figure rather than on the Temple cult. For the rabbis, Hannah is one of the great biblical examples of a person who prays with deep intensity. The way Hannah prayed is described in the *Tanach* and used as a paradigm for prayer by the rabbis. We say the *Tefillah* today just as Hannah uttered her prayer. As Hannah said her prayer, silently moving her lips and with great intensity, so do we say the *Amidah*. Of course, the adjuration to refrain from the prayer while intoxicated is a continuation of our theme: we must approach prayer soberly, seriously, and with a heart ready to relate to God.

Where does piety fit into the system of *mitzvot*? What is its value? The rabbis assume that the pious individual is *already* observing the *mitzvot*. Given that assumption, the following hierarchy applies:

GEMARA (32b): Rabbi Eleazar said, "Prayer is greater even than good deeds, for there was no one greater in good deeds than Moses our Teacher, and he was answered only in prayer, as it says, 'Speak no more unto Me' (Deuteronomy 3:26), and immediately afterward, 'Get you up unto the top of Pisgah' (Deuteronomy 3:27)."

Rabbi Eleazar also said, "Fasting is greater than charity. What is the reason? One is performed with a man's money, the other with his body."

This *sugya* may seem an unusual departure from the norms of the rabbis. We would expect them to say that good deeds are more efficacious than prayer and charity more efficacious than fasting (consider, for example, the text from Chapter 1, p. 6b, which said, "the merit of a fast day lies in the charity dispensed"). Yet in this *sugya* we find the exact opposite. This is yet another instance of the Gemara viewing an issue from more than one perspective at the same time. In Chapter 1, we are exploring the basic nature of our relationship with God. In this chapter, we are examining a special dimension within that relationship. Eleazar assumes that the person of whom he speaks is already committed to the basic relationship, is *already* giving charity on a fast day. *Within* that category of persons, fasting is more efficacious than charity. Obviously, the people Eleazar is referring to will give the charity *and* fast.

Rabbi Eleazar uses a *drashah* to support his contentions. Moses, unrivaled in good deeds, wanted to see the Land of Israel before he died. He prayed to God, "I pray, please let me see that good land which is across the Jordan" (Deuteronomy 3:25). It is the only then, *after* Moses prays, that God answers, "Go up to the top of the Pisgah and raise your eyes in every direction and look to the west, the north, the south, and the east and see with your own eyes" (Deuteronomy 3:27).

Rabbi Eleazar asserts that prayer is more efficacious than good deeds, and fasting more than charity. His criterion for determining these rankings seems to be that the more inward a behavior—the more *self* it takes—the more efficacious it is. Good deeds and charity are meritorious acts, but they might be done mechanically, not tapping into the most deeply felt part of our relationship with God. For that, we must involve our physical and spiritual selves. This is the essence of piety.

Such piety is seen in its most potent form in the willingness to brave physical danger for the sake of our relationship with God.

> **GEMARA (32b):** Our Rabbis taught: It is a story about a certain pious man who was praying by the roadside. An officer came by and greeted him, and he did not return his greeting. So he waited for him till he had finished his prayer. After he had finished his prayer he said to him, "Fool! Is it not written in your Torah, 'Only take heed to yourself and keep your soul diligently' (Deuteronomy 4:9)? And it is also written, 'Take you therefore good heed unto your souls' (Deuteronomy 4:15)? When I greeted you why did you not return my greeting? If I had cut off your head with my sword, who would have demanded satisfaction for your blood from me?"
>
> He said to him, "Wait, and let my words appease you. If you had been standing before an earthly king and your friend had come and given you greeting, would you (33a) have returned it?"
>
> He said to him, "No."
>
> "And if you had returned his greeting, what would they have done to you?"
>
> He said, "They would have cut off my head with the sword."
> He said to him, "Have we not here then an *a fortiori* argument: If [you would have behaved] in this way when standing before a king of flesh and blood who is here today and tomorrow is in the grave, how much more so I [should I act the same way], when standing before the supreme King of Kings, the Holy One, blessed be He, who lives and endures for all eternity?"
>
> The officer was immediately appeased, and the pious man returned to his home in peace.
>
> "Even if a snake is wound round his foot he should not break off." Rav Sheshet said, "This applies only to a serpent, but if it is a scorpion, he breaks off."

The rabbis demand an extraordinary level of concentration during prayer in this *sugya*. Again, they are showing us two sides of a multifaceted problem. There is a minimum standard of concentration (*din*) and an optimum standard (*lifnim mishurat hadin*). That optimal standard is the subject of this chapter. When pious people pray, they already feel as though they are standing before a king, and it is on this sovereign that all their attention is focused.

This is not merely a fanciful point or an extreme position. Rather, it is an important philosophical comment on power, self-control, and intention during prayer. Imagine that you are standing in a synagogue saying the *Amidah* when the president of the United States walks into the sanctuary. You would be hard pressed not to stop praying, turn around, and greet him. But a truly pious person would be so deeply engrossed in prayer that he or she would not even notice the presence of such a leader. It is a question of priorities: who comes first with us—those who exercise temporal authority on earth, or the One who truly controls our lives? Only the pious are not fooled into believing that the rich and powerful truly control anything.

Later commentators asked how this pious man could have kept praying, since we are allowed to interrupt our prayers if we are in danger. They explain that since the officer greeted him and then waited, apparently understanding what he was doing, the pious man was confident that the officer would not hurt him while he finished his prayer.

When our lives are truly threatened, preserving life takes precedence over piety. If a snake is wound around one's leg, one does not stop praying unless, adds the *halachah*, it seems that the snake is about to bite. However, if a scorpion is on one's leg, one may interrupt one's prayers, since the rabbis deemed a scorpion more likely to bite than a snake.

Now we move to the other side of the coin of piety: apostasy. If piety is total devotion to God, apostasy is the total abandonment of the relationship with God. No one in rabbinic literature more clearly represents this phenomenon than Elisha ben Abuya. Even when he is not mentioned by name, the influence of this rabbi's loss of faith is felt.

MISHNAH (33b): If one [in praying] says "May Your mercies extend to a bird's nest" (see Deuteronomy 22:6), "Be Your name mentioned for well-doing," or "We give thanks, we give thanks," he is silenced.

GEMARA: Granted, he is silenced if he says "we give thanks, we give thanks", because he seems to be acknowledging two Powers. And [if he says], "Be Your name mentioned for well-doing," similarly, because this implies, for the good only and not for the bad, and we have learnt: A person is obligated to bless God for the evil as he blesses Him for the good. But [what is the reason for silencing him if he says], "Your mercies extend to the bird's nest"? Two Amoraim in the West, Rabbi Jose bar Avin and Rabbi Jose bar Zevida, give different answers. One said, it is because he creates jealousy among God's creatures. The other, because he presents the measures taken by the Holy One, blessed be He, as springing from compassion, whereas they are but decrees.

Gnosticism, the religious system of two gods, an evil one and a good one, was anathema to the rabbis, as we see in this mishnah. Each of the three prohibited statements reminds them in some way of apostasy. One can see this easily in the latter two statements. If one praises God only for the good, it might imply that there is another god responsible for the evil in this world. Likewise, saying "we give thanks" twice might imply the existence of two gods.

But what of the third statement mentioned in the Gemara? It refers to Deuteronomy 22:6–7, which states, "If, along the road, you chance upon a bird's nest, in any tree or on the ground, with fledglings or eggs and the mother sitting over the fledglings or on the eggs, do not take the mother together with her young. Let the mother go, and take only the young, in order that you may fare well and have a long life." This commandment and the commandment to honor one's father and mother (Deuteronomy 5:16) are the only two commandments in the Torah which explicitly mention that their reward is a long life.

It is told (in *Hullin* 142a) that once Elisha ben Abuya, a second-century *Tanna*, saw a boy and his father on the road. The father asked his son to climb a tree, shoo the mother bird away from her eggs, and bring the eggs down to him. The son did as he was bidden and drove the mother bird away from her nest, but then, instead of being rewarded with long life for honoring his father and showing mercy to the bird, he fell to his death. When Elisha ben Abuya saw this he uttered what has become the ultimate apostasy in Judaism: *"Leit din v'leit dayan"* (There is no judgment and there is no Judge). Thereafter, Elisha ben Abuya turned to idol worship. Thus, these verses regarding the bird's nest became important to the rabbis, as a general concept to both defend (the One God rewards and punishes) and avoid, as we see in this *sugya*.

There is a hint at the rabbis' underlying concern in the reasons they give for banning mention of the bird's nest in prayer. Both their rationales—that it implies that God favors one creature over others or that God is not a fair and constant judge—are aimed at disproving Elisha ben Abuya's apostasy. "There *is* a Judge of judgment," the rabbis seem to be saying, "And it is the One God. But we will avoid even giving the appearance that God is an unfair judge and ban an essentially beautiful and merciful edict from our prayers, since it has come to mean exactly the opposite: that God is arbitrary and cruel; no Judge at all."

The rabbis' explanation of apparent injustice was that goodness would be rewarded and evil punished in a life after death. The rabbis explained the existence of evil by maintaining that all suffering by the righteous in this world will be repaid in the world to come. These sufferings are called *yisurim shel ahavah*, "afflictions of love." God sends them to the righteous in order that they should overcome these sufferings and so earn even greater rewards in the world to come. Although the rabbis could never completely understand the suffering of the righteous, they still maintained their belief in God's just and merciful nature.

However, Elisha ben Abuya obviously had lost his belief in a life after death and faith in the justness of God's system. He therefore abandoned the Jewish religion entirely. What of modern Jews who find themselves in Elisha ben Abuya's position? Does the Jewish system of belief work only when we believe in a life after death? No. Many Jews are able to practice Judaism and study Torah without such a belief. Especially after the Holocaust, it is difficult to believe in basic goodness and fairness as overriding organizing principles in our world. On the other hand, if we accept that we are human beings with finite minds that are incapable of grasping the order that the Infinite Mind produces, we may still be able to remain within the Jewish system of belief. Every person must struggle with this problem and come to his or her own resolution of it.

Our chapter, and the whole first section of this tractate, end with a *nechemtah*, a promise of redemption. If we have given up our faith, can we retrieve it? Yes, is the comforting answer. Not only can we retrieve it, but we may even come closer to God than one who never lost faith.

GEMARA (34b): Rabbi Abbahu said, "In the place where penitents stand even the wholly righteous cannot stand, as it says, 'Peace, peace to him that was far and to him that is near' (Isaiah 57:19)—to him that was far first, and then to him that is near."

And Rabbi Johanan told to you, "What is meant by 'far'? One who, from the beginning, was far from transgression. And what is meant by 'near'? That he was once near to transgression and now has gone far from it." . . .

Rav Kahana said, "I consider one who prays in a valley impertinent."

Rav Kahana also said, "I consider one who openly recounts his sins impertinent, since it is said, 'Happy is he whose transgression is forgiven, whose sin is covered' (Psalms 32:1)."

The rabbis assure us that no matter how far we may have strayed, there is always a way back to God. Not only will God take us back, but we will be more treasured than those who never strayed. Naturally, the rabbis want to qualify this statement, lest it encourage people to stray, but it is still a message of hope: God is forgiving, merciful, and loving. The last note of the chapter maintains the theme of the whole: piety, even confessing one's sins, is a private matter. We should not do it in a valley, since people would constantly pass by and either interrupt or overhear us. We should make our confession in a private, secluded spot. We should not expect congratulations for having sinned and done *teshuvah*—just forgiveness.

This idea of not being proud of one's sins directly contradicts much of contemporary American culture, which is devoted to publicly confessing and examining the ways we have sinned, overeaten, or abused ourselves or those we love. This behavior glorifies sin, and that is not what the rabbis wanted. They did not even want to glorify piety! They knew that the strongest relationships are those that do not need validation from the outside world, those in which problems and conflicts, as well as joys, can be shared in a private, loving circle. Ideally, that is what our relationship with God provides.

With this *sugya*, the first major section of our tractate draws to a close. We have explored the *Shema* and *Amidah*. We have defined our basic relationship with God and examined what interferes with that relationship and how to deal with that interference. We have examined our places as individuals within that relationship, and we have defined how we can improve the relationship, or forsake it. The second half of our tractate moves to a different level: how do our desires, our intellects, and our encounters with the extraordinary contribute to this relationship? We move from the more direct contact outlined in the first five chapters to a less direct, less regular kind of contact in the last four chapters.

6

Consecrating Our Desires

S ometimes the most critical issues in a relationship are worked out in the details: the "thank you" said, or forgotten, week after week, year after year; the communication that happens, or doesn't, over the family dinner table. This is the realm of our relationship with God that the second section of our tractate explores. In it we will examine ways to relate to God in our day-to-day lives. These moments of connection with God occur outside the synagogue and apart from scheduled moments of devotion. We relate to God through our appetites and desires (Chapter 6); by placing ourselves in the chain of tradition (that is, by internalizing the rabbis' way of thinking (Chapter 7); through our intellects (Chapter 8); and through astonishing experiences that seem to come from a realm outside of everyday reality (Chapter 9).

This division of the tractate is borne out in its literary composition. You will recall that our very first mishnah in Chapter 1 began, "*From when* do we recite the *Shema*?" Because the *Shema* and *Tefillah* are to be said at specific times, it is logical that the section concerning them begins with the word *when*, emphasizing the importance of time. In this second section of the tractate, time is not a determining factor: the blessings we will examine depend on actions that need not be done at a specific time (for example eating) and on some phenomena that are quite unpredictable (such as earthquakes or lightning). So it is logical that this section begins "*How* do we bless?" Significantly, Chapters 1 and 6 are the only chapters in this tractate that begin with questions.

Judaism is *passionate* monotheism. Therefore, passionate feelings and desires are used to fuel our relationship with God. Chapter 6 demonstrates ways in which we can consecrate our desires. Here the sages use principles already established in the first five chapters to guide our prayerful behavior when we are not in a specifically worshipful setting. *Berachot* such as those over food, wine, pleasant smells, and trees blossoming in the spring serve several functions. They not only consecrate our desires, but they also transfer ownership of the things we enjoy from God to us. Having made this transfer, the *berachot* also help us express our gratitude to God for that which we enjoy. Of course, all these functions serve the main relationship with God, a passionate monotheism whose systematic expression extends to every area of an individual's existence.

The chapter begins by describing the blessings we say before eating food.

> **MISHNAH (35a):** How do we bless fruit [before we eat it]? Over fruit of the tree one says, " . . . who creates the fruit of the tree"; except for wine, over which one says, " . . . who creates the fruit of the vine."
>
> Over the fruit of the ground one says, " . . . who creates the fruit of the ground"; except over bread, over which one says, "who brings forth bread from the earth."

The blessings we say over foods remind us from whence they came. It is interesting that the rabbis composed special blessings for wine and bread that praise God for creating them. After all, bread does not come from the earth, nor wine from the vine. Each of them requires human effort to create the finished product. Why, then, these special *berachot*? Perhaps because wine and bread epitomize the Jewish view of what we need to survive: nourishment for the body (bread) and the soul (wine). In addition, they are the materials out of which we build consecrated moments. As such, they occupy a special place among the foods we consume. Just as grain and grapes are transformed to make bread and wine, so do bread and wine transform our moments into something higher and more valuable.

What purpose do the benedictions serve? The following *sugya* brings out two of the functions of the *berachot:* (1) they help us remember we are part of a community that includes God; and (2) they remind us that the earth belongs to God: we are guests here and should behave with the grace and care of guests who are well treated.

> **GEMARA (35a):** Our Rabbis taught: It is forbidden for a person to enjoy anything of this world without a benediction, and anyone who enjoys anything of this world without a benediction, commits sacrilege. What is the remedy? He should consult a wise man. What will the wise man do for him? He has already committed the offense!
>
> "Rather," said Rava, "let him go to a wise man to begin with, and he will teach him the blessings, in order that he should not commit sacrilege."
>
> Rav Judah said in the name of Samuel, "To enjoy anything of this world without a benediction is like making use of things consecrated to heaven, since it says, 'The earth is the Lord's and the fullness thereof' (Psalms 24:1)."
>
> Rabbi Levi contrasted two texts. It is written, "The earth is the Lord's and the fullness thereof," and it is also written, "The heavens are the heavens of the Lord, but the earth He has given to the children of men" (Psalms 115:16)! There is no contradiction: in the one case it is before a blessing has been said (35b); in the other case, afterward.
>
> Rabbi Hanina bar Papa said, "Anyone who enjoys this world without a benediction, it is as if he robbed the Holy One, blessed be He, and the congregation of Israel, as it says, 'Whoso robs his father or his mother and says, "It is no transgression," the same is the companion of a destroyer' (Proverbs 28:24) And 'father' is none other than the Holy One blessed be He, as it says, 'Is not He your father that has gotten you' (Deuteronomy 32:6) and 'mother' is none other than the community of Israel, as it says, 'Hear, my son, the instruction of your father, and forsake not the teaching of your mother' (Proverbs 1:8)."

The benedictions take our desires, a potentially destructive force to our souls, and turn them into prayer. This is the genius of the rabbinic system: it does not try to eradicate desires, an impossible task in any case, or even denigrate them. Rather, it seeks to use the energy our desires engender and redirect it toward high purpose. *Kol Haneshama*, the Reconstructionist prayer book, quotes a Hasidic story that beautifully expresses this concept: "The Baal Shem Tov had a method for dealing with distractions, especially sexual ones. If you can't get that person out of your thoughts, remember that beauty is a reflection of God's image. Redirect that energy towards God" (p. 81). Blessings convert desires that, unrestrained, could hurt us and those around us into holy, safe energy.

And how can we help ourselves be more aware of our desires, control them more fully, and use them in a holier way? By consulting someone who has already learned how to do so. In this case, the rabbis recommend a wise man, but it could be anyone who can serve as a role model of self-control. This, after all, is what makes self-help groups so successful. It is the ability of those who have overcome the temptations we face to inspire us and teach us to do the same.

We note a tension in this *sugya* between the ideas that everything belongs to God and that God gave the earth to us to enjoy. Rabbi Levi harmonizes the two concepts: *berachot* are the means by which we transfer the objects of our desires from God to ourselves. But *berachot* serve more than even this function: they do something for the Jewish people. If, as a people, we allow ourselves to fulfill our appetites without appreciating that they have an impact on others, then we may become irresponsible in the fulfillment of those appetites. We may forget, for instance, that the land into which we dump our garbage is the land from which our food grows. The rabbis want us to act as parents to the earth and to ourselves. Parents want their children to fulfill their desires *and* control them. It is not that we are to refrain from enjoying things. We must simply do so within reason, knowing that no legitimate pleasure is denied us in this system of passionate monotheism.

Blessings over enjoyment, *Birkot Hanehanim*, serve our relationship with God in one further way. They help us change, or maintain, our spiritual course on a minute-by-minute basis. If we have been following a hurtful or sinful path, the blessings that we say throughout the day may help us turn and start on a more righteous one. The next *sugya* demonstrates how to sustain such a change.

> **GEMARA (40a):** Rabbi Zera, and some say, Rabbi Hanina bar Papa, further said: Come and see how the character of the Holy One blessed be He is not like the character of flesh and blood. It is characteristic of flesh and blood to be able to put something into an empty vessel but not into a full one. But the Holy One blessed be He is not so. He puts more into a full vessel, but not into an empty one; for it says, "And He said, 'If hearkening you will hearken' Exodus (15:26)," implying if you hearken [once] you will go on hearkening, and if not, you will not hearken. Another explanation is: If you hearken to the old, you will hearken to the new, but if your heart turns away, you will not hear anymore.

Not all of our desires are for material goods or pleasures of the flesh. We also have appetites for intellectual stimulation and piety. These appetites are like many others: the more we have of what we desire, the more we want. God facilitates our ever-increasing appetite for goodness and learning. This is sometimes called *hitlahavut*, "a burning desire for good," and it characterizes those who are on fire with their love of Torah.

Our tradition teaches that one *mitzvah* begets another and one transgression begets another. In other words, once we choose a path to follow, toward righteousness or toward evil, our motion perpetuates itself. We may have only a few opportunities to change our direction, and we must be ready to exploit them when they occur. For example, the Israelites were enslaved in Egypt for 210 years. They had one opportunity to change their lot from slavery to freedom when Moses came to lead them out of Egypt, and they took it.

The rabbis chose to illustrate their point about using opportunities for change with a passage from the Exodus story. Rabbi Zera (or Rabbi Hanina bar Papa) are playing on a special grammatical form in the Hebrew that conveys intensity through a double use of the emphasized word. (This is the first time in the whole *Tanach* that this Hebrew grammatical form is used with the root, *shin-mem-ayin*, to hear.) In the verse just cited (Exodus 15:26), the people of Israel have just crossed the Red Sea and sung the Song of the Sea, celebrating God's saving power in their lives. Afterward, God commands them to hearken diligently to God's voice. Significantly, the rabbis chose to illustrate their point with the root of the word *Shema*.

Egypt traditionally symbolizes desires that are not controlled, a preoccupation with death rather than life, and slavery. So God's first command to the Jewish people after they have left that mind-set behind is to adopt a system of discipline and life, learning and joy. In other words, they are to experience their deep emotions within the chain of tradition. Simple fervor is not enough, as the following *sugya* shows. It must be fervor framed and guided by Jewish values.

> **GEMARA (40b):** If one saw a loaf of bread and said, "How fine a loaf this is! Blessed be the Omnipresent Who created it!" he has fulfilled his obligation [to say a blessing over the bread]. So said Rabbi Meir.
>
> Rabbi Jose says, "Anyone who alters the formula for benedictions laid down by the Sages has not fulfilled his obligation."

We can think of our emotions and desires as a liquid. The vessel into which we pour that liquid will contain the fluid and give it shape. That is the function of the blessings. The blessings are the necessary, stable counterpart to our volatile, spontaneous emotions and experiences. The only remaining question is, just how rigid must the vessel be that contains our spontaneity? In general, Judaism devises the most minimal ritual framework for occasions when great emotional and spiritual powers are at work. No elaborate liturgy is necessary at a funeral: the impetus for prayer is directly at hand. Likewise, at a wedding, we need only the lightest touch, the most minimal ritual, to frame the emotions of joy, fear, and hope. Similarly, when we are about to eat, we need only a minimal ritual, the one-line *berachah*, to express our thanks and change our desire from mere want to an affirmation of our relationship with God.

The formula "Blessed are You, O Lord our God, Ruler of the Universe, who . . ." expresses much of our relationship with God. It affirms God as Judge (Eloheinu), as Merciful One (Adonai), as the transcendent Creator of vast order (Ruler of the Universe), as the immanent God who brings bread from the earth and fruit from the trees, and as the God of the Jewish people (who sanctifies us with *mitzvot*). No matter how powerful this formula is, if it hinders our expression of gratitude to God rather than giving that gratitude wings, then it has not performed its functions. Better to be a little spontaneous and sincere in prayer than formulaic and without intention.

The important role desire can play in giving intention to prayer is seen in the next *sugya*.

> **MISHNAH (40b):** And over anything which does not grow from the earth one says, "by whose word all things exist"...If one has several varieties before him, Rabbi Judah says that if there is among them something of the seven kinds, he makes the blessing over that, but the sages say that he may make the blessing over any of them that he wishes.

> **GEMARA (41a):** "If one had several varieties before him," Ulla said. "Opinions differ only in the case where the blessings [over the several varieties of food] are the same. In such a case Rabbi Judah holds that belonging to the seven kinds is of more importance, while the Rabbis hold that being better liked is of more importance. But where they do not all have the same benediction, all agree that a blessing is to be said first on one [variety of food which he likes best] and then on the other."

This *sugya* clearly demonstrates the theme of this chapter. Ordinarily, we might expect the rabbis to use the fact that something is mentioned in the Torah as a basis for their rulings. For example, in Deuteronomy 8:8, God promises to bring us to a land of "wheat and barley, of vines, figs, and pomegranates, a land of olive trees and honey." Because these seven species are mentioned in the Torah, we might think that they ought to be blessed first. However, the rabbis clearly state that we are to bless that which we like best first. Why? Because our *desire* is the holy thing in this case, even more than the holiest of arbitrary orders—that is, being mentioned in the Torah.

However, we must never forget that desires can be made holy only if they are controlled. We must be careful lest we give even the *appearance* of not having our appetites under our command.

GEMARA (43b): Our Rabbis taught: Six things are unbecoming for a scholar. He should not go abroad scented; he should not go out by night alone; he should not go abroad in patched sandals; he should not converse with a woman in the street; he should not take a set meal in the company of ignorant persons (*amei ha-arets*); and he should not be the last to enter the *Beit HaMidrash*. Some add that he should not take long strides nor carry himself haughtily (quite uprightly, or stiffly).

"He should not go abroad scented." Rabbi Abba the son of Rabbi Hiyya bar Abba said in the name of Rabbi Johanan, "This applies only to a place where people are suspected of pederasty." Rav Sheshet said, "This applies only to [the scenting of] one's clothes; but [perfuming] the body removes the perspiration." Rav Papa said, "The hair is on the same footing as clothes"; others, however, say, "as the body."

"He should not go out at night alone," so as not to arouse suspicion. This is the case only if he has no fixed appointment; but if he has a fixed appointment, people know that he is going to his appointment.

"He should not go abroad in patched sandals." This supports Rabbi Hiyya bar Abba; for Rabbi Hiyya bar Abba said, "It is unseemly for a scholar to go abroad in patched sandals." Is that so? Rabbi Hiyya bar Abba did go out [in such sandals]. Mar Zutra the son of Rav Nahman said, "He was speaking of one patch on top of another patch. And this applies only to the uppers, but if it is on the sole, there is no objection. On the upper, too, this applies only [when it is worn] on the public road; but in the house there is no objection. Further, this is the case only in summer; but in the rainy season there is no objection."

"He should not converse with a woman in the street." Rav Hisda said, "Even with his wife." It has been taught similarly, "Even if she is his wife, and even if she is his daughter, and even if she is his sister, because not everyone knows who are his female relatives."

"He should not take a set meal with ignorant persons." What is the reason? Perhaps he will be drawn into their ways.

"He should not be last to enter the *Beit HaMidrash*," lest he be called a transgressor.

Some add that he should not take long strides because the Master said, ''Long strides take away one five-hundredth of a person's eyesight.'' What is the remedy? He can restore it by [drinking] the sanctification wine of Sabbath eve (see tractate *Shabbat* 113b).

"Nor should he carry himself haughtily (quite uprightly)," since the Master said, "If one walks haughtily even for four cubits, it is as if he pushed against the heels of the Divine Presence, since it is written, 'The whole earth is full of His glory' (Isaiah 6:3)."

For the rabbis, a scholar was a role model. He had to exemplify in his life the highest ethical standards. He therefore had to avoid even the appearance of not controlling his desires. We saw in Chapter 5 that the rabbis highly valued inward devotion. Here, we learn that appearances are also important. A scholar must not give the impression that he does not control his desires for sexual gratification, money, and sleep.

He must even control his desire to achieve and his pride in his accomplishments. If a scholar rushed around, it indicated that he might have been out of control in two ways. First, he may have been distracted by his desires and now must hurry to make up for lost time. Second, perhaps he was taking long strides, intensely thinking about Torah but ignoring the people he passed along the way. This is not the path of righteousness. Even our desire for learning must be tempered with an awareness of the world around us. That is why the rabbis prescribe the *Shabbat* wine for such a man: let him rest, relax, and learn to enjoy life and relationships.

The rabbis wanted us to protect the learning embodied within us. We must take care not to sully it in any way. We should appear neither flamboyantly dressed nor too poorly dressed. We should not give the impression that we do not control our appetites for sex (either heterosexual or homosexual). We should not endanger that learning by fraternizing with those who do not control their passions and who might urge us to lower our standards. We should take care that our actions are consistent with our learning. However, the rabbis also warn us not to hold ourselves too uprightly: we must guard against becoming self-righteous, prissy individuals.

The desire for learning is like the desire for food in some ways. It is a hunger we fill each day. But learning, unlike food, once internalized, stays with us. Over food, we need say only one, quick blessing; but we must guard the learning within us continuously.

7

Who Counts?
Who Belongs in a Group?

W ho's in and who's out? Who is picked to be on that committee? In the executive suite? And why were they picked? These questions and their answers, form a big part of one's identity. They are no less important in Jewish life. Who belongs in a Jewish group that assembles to pray? People who are able, by their position in life, to have an intense, direct relationship with God. And who are valued most in that group? Those who maintain that relationship most richly. The background against which we discuss these issues of group membership is the etiquette of a meal. Why do we explore these issues in this context rather than in the setting of synagogue services? First, in the synagogue service, the delineation between those who are included and those who are not may be more clear cut than it would be in the context of the home. In addition, more people would need guidelines to enable them to decide whom to include in the invitation to say grace after meals than would need guidelines for the conduct of synagogue services. Finally, people may have said grace as a group more often than they said the *Shema* or *Tefillah* as a group. Eating is usually a family or communal activity, whereas praying need not be.

We have already examined, in Chapter 6, how one should say grace before a meal. These blessings are *DeRabbanan*, ordained by the rabbis. However, the main grace, called *Birkat HaMazon*, is said *after* the meal. This grace after the meal is *De-*

Oraita, from the Torah, for it states in Deuteronomy 8:10, "And you shall eat and be satisfied, and bless the Lord Your God for the good land which God has given you." Of course, the form *Birkat HaMazon* took was determined by the rabbis. It begins with the *zimmun*, an invitation to say grace which may only be said if three qualifying people are present. If ten or more qualifying people partook of the meal, the word *Eloheinu*, "Our God," is added to this invitation. The following blessings are then recited:

1. Thanks for food.
2. Thanks for the Land of Israel.
3. Plea for mercy upon Jerusalem and the destroyed Temple.
4. Various additional blessings and verses of praise.

Additions for Shabbat, festivals, and other holidays are added when appropriate, just as they are added into the *Tefillah*.

We begin with a description of who must invite others to say grace and who may not do so.

MISHNAH (45a): If three persons have eaten together, they are obligated to invite one another [to say grace]. One who has eaten *demai*, or first tithe from which *terumah* has been removed, or second tithe or food belonging to the Sanctuary that has been redeemed, or an attendant who has eaten as much as an olive or a Cutean may be counted [in the three who are needed for the invitation].

One who has eaten *tevel* or first tithe from which the *terumah* has not been removed, or second tithe or sanctified food which has not been redeemed, or an attendant who has eaten less than the quantity of an olive, or a gentile, may not be counted [in the three who are needed for the invitation].

Women, children, and slaves may not be counted [in the three]. How much [must one have eaten] to count [in the three]? As much as an olive; Rabbi Judah says as much as an egg.

GEMARA: Whence is this derived? Rav Assi says, "Because Scriptures says, 'O magnify ye [two] the Lord with me [one], and let us exalt His name together' (Psalms 34:4)."

Rabbi Abbahu derives it from here: "For I [one] proclaim the name of the Lord, ascribe ye [two] greatness unto our God" (Deuteronomy 32:3).

What qualifies an individual to join in the *zimmun* before grace? He must be a free, adult man who has joined the Jewish covenant with God in some way, and who has eaten an olive's worth (approximately 0.9 fluid ounces or 28 cubic centimeters) of food that is permitted to him. If any of these factors are missing, the person may not be included in the *zimmun*.

What makes food fit to eat? It must have all the necessary "Jewish taxes" taken out of it already (see the Glossary for descriptions of these "taxes"). If a portion of the food consumed is owed to charity, the Temple cult, or the priests, then it is not fit to be blessed. It is almost as if this food had a lien on it.

The rabbis mention diverse categories of persons in regard to *zimmun*. The rabbis permitted Cuteans (Samaritans) to be counted for *zimmun*, although later generations excluded them. The Samaritans punctiliously followed the part of the Written Torah they accepted but ignored the rest of it, and the Oral one. Since Cuteans accepted the obligation to say grace after meals, the rabbis presumed they would fulfill their obligation punctiliously.

One might wonder why the rabbis even mention a Gentile. The Gemara explains that the Gentile spoken of here is a man in the process of converting to Judaism who has been circumcised but has not immersed himself in the *mikveh*. Until he completes his conversion with the ritual immersion, they do not consider him a Jew.

Women may not invite men or slaves to say grace with them, even though, as we noted in Chapter 3, they *are* obligated to say the grace itself. The exclusion of women from this *mitzvah* does not fit logically within the system of limitations placed on women regarding the *mitzvot*. Women are excluded from leading prayers in public because they are not obligated to do positive, time-bound commandments, and thus (presumably) they would not perform them with the same intention as men. However, women *are* obligated to say *Birkat HaMazon*. Yet they are still denied the privilege and responsibility of leading the invitation to say grace. This case illustrates a basic truth, summarized by Rachel Biale (1984) in her book *Women and Jewish Law*.

> Enumerating the exceptions to the rule that women are exempt from all time-bound positive mitzvot raises serious doubts that historically this principle governed which mitzvot women fulfilled and which they did not. Rather than an *a priori* rule about exemptions of women from certain mitzvot, what probably occurred historically was a gradual evolution of daily practice and communal customs which allowed women not to perform certain mitzvot. Eventually the customs acquired the force of law and the halakhic justification probably emerged initially on a case-by-case basis. The principle that women are exempt from all time-bound positive mitzvot and obligated in all others was probably an after-the-fact attempt to explain and systematize the reality that women did not perform all the mitzvot equally with men. [p. 17]

If we were to use the true criteria that the rabbis developed to determine who belongs in a group for prayer, we might come up with very different roles for women and men to play today. As we have noted, group membership in this situation basically depends on three factors: (1) having enjoyed food that we may legitimately eat, (2) wanting to give thanks for that food within the context of our continuing relationship with God, and (3) having the Jewish competence to lead the *zimmun* and *Birkat HaMazon*. Many women fill these three requirements today, as they must have in the rabbinic era.

What, then, prevented the rabbis from seeing women as the equals of men in this situation? It may have been the time-consuming nature of women's household duties that disqualified them, for the rabbis make special rules for the woman who is an *ishah chashuvah*, "an important woman"—that is, a woman wealthy enough presumably to have servants to do her work for her, thus freeing her to perform *mitzvot*. Such women are frequently grouped with men. For example, the *ishah chashuvah* must recline during a seder, while an "unimportant" woman in her husband's house is not obligated to recline (*Pesachim* 108a). An *ishah chashuvah* is as subject to certain harmful spirits, as is a man (*Pesachim* 110b). Thus, it seems, any woman who has free time due to few responsibilities may be considered an *ishah chashuvah*. Today, it could be argued, many women fall into the category of *ishah chashuvah* and should be accorded that status in terms of the system of *mitzvot*.

> **GEMARA (45b):** Come and hear: women by themselves invite one another, and slaves by themselves invite one another, but women, slaves and children together even if they desire to invite one another may not do so.... Now a hundred women are no better than two men [for the purposes of saying the *zimmun*], yet it says, "Women by themselves invite one another and slaves by themselves invite one another"? There is a special reason there, because each has a mind. If that is so, look at the next clause: "Women and slaves together, even though they desire to invite one another may not do so." Why not? Each has a mind! There is a special reason in that case, because it might lead to immorality.

What ambivalence the rabbis felt about women and Jewish slaves! Were they people with complete status within the Jewish community? No. But they were clearly some kind of persons. Therefore, the rabbis' task became the defining of the limitations placed on these persons' membership in the community. The rabbis' confusion is seen here. If a group of three of more women eat together with no men or slaves present, then they can lead each other in the *zimmun*. Why? Because they meet all the criteria for saying the *zimmun*: they have eaten fit food to be blessed, they are obligated to say the blessing by their relationship with God, and they are Jewishly competent enough to say the *zimmun* and *Birkat HaMazon*. However, if they combine their group with a group of slaves, none of them may say the *zimmun* for fear of "immorality."

While this objection may seem farfetched, it is not. Prayer and study build self-esteem, intimacy, and love and make those with whom we pray and study more attractive. Gems displayed on black velvet under bright lights may appear far more desirable than the same gems viewed in harsh sunlight. By placing men and women together in a situation that sets them off to their best advantage (prayer or study), each can seem more attractive to the other.

Perhaps the rabbis did not believe that women and slaves could have as close a relationship with God as did free, Jewish men, because they assumed that women and slaves did not stand directly in the chain of tradition: they did not learn mishnah and gemara. If only they had not made this assumption! If they had clearly stated that learning and valuing the tradition are the true criteria for group membership, rather than gender or slavery status, they would have more accurately stated their true views.

Among those qualified to say *zimmun*, there is a further hierarchy regarding who is *most* qualified.

> **GEMARA (46a):** Rabbi Zera once fell ill. Rabbi Abbahu visited him, and took upon himself [the following vow], "If the little one with scorched legs recovers, I will make a feast for the Rabbis." He did recover, and he made a feast for all the Rabbis. When the time came to begin the meal, he said to Rabbi Zera, "Let the Master make the blessing [ha-motzi] for us!" He said to him, "Does the Master not accept the dictum of Rabbi Johanan, that the host should break bread?" So he [Rabbi Abbahu] commenced the meal [and broke the bread for them].
>
> When the time came for saying grace he said to him [Rabbi Zera], "Let the Master say grace for us!" He said to him, "Does the Master not accept the ruling of Rav Huna from Babylon, who said that the one who breaks bread says grace?" Whose view then did he [Rabbi Abbahu] accept? That expressed by Rabbi Johanan in the name of Rabbi Simeon ben Yohai: The host breaks bread and the guest says grace. The host breaks bread so that he should do so generously, and the guest says grace so that he should bless the host. How does he bless him? "May it be God's will that our host should never be ashamed in this world nor disgraced in the next world."

Who should say grace? Apparently, it depends on what you hold to be more important—expressing feelings of welcome and thanks or maintaining continuity during a prayer event. The custom of the Land of Israel favors the former; the Babylonian the latter. The custom of the Land of Israel mandates that the host say grace so that as he breaks the bread and passes out pieces of it to his guests, he may do so generously, inviting them in prayer and in deed to enjoy his hospitality. The Babylonian custom emphasizes continuity in prayer. The person who thanked God before eating the food must finish the cycle and thank God for the food after eating it. In this case, the halachah holds that expressing feelings in prayer is more important than continuity. Once more, true intention is a very important part of sincere prayer. Those who have emotions that can be best expressed in prayer take precedence over the other persons in the group.

Rabbi Zera seems to have been a shy and retiring man, more interested in his internal struggle for righteousness than in public honors. Of him it is written in *Baba Metsia* 85a:

> When Rabbi Zera emigrated to the Land of Israel he fasted . . . a hundred days that the fire of Gehenna might be powerless against him. Every thirty days he used to examine himself [to see if he were fireproof]. He would heat the oven, ascend, and sit therein, but the fire had no power against him. One day, however, the Rabbis cast an [envious] eye upon him, and his legs were singed, whereafter he was called, "short and leg-singed."

Zera was obviously a man who would have preferred spending time in deep contemplation rather than at banquets. He may even have been embarrassed to have a dinner in his honor, for he tries, through his knowledge of the different customs of the Land of Israel and Babylonia, to avoid saying the blessings before and after the meal. At the beginning of the evening he urges Abbahu to follow the custom of the Land of Israel and Abbahu complies. This is expected: the dinner is taking place in the Land of Israel, and Abbahu was Rabbi Johanan's student as well. At the end, Zera appeals to the custom of a Babylonian sage that would excuse him from saying grace. Thus, Zera finds a way to accommodate his shyness through the halachah.

This story shows us how we must balance our need to be—or our need to *avoid* being—the center of attention with our need to cultivate an eagerness to praise God. If some less pious person had spoken as Rabbi Zera had, his statement would appear to be an expression of a reluctance to pray. Here, however, it is an expression of Rabbi Zera's private piety. While this may have been a legitimate expression of his nature, the Gemara generally urges us to accept the opportunity to lead a congregation in prayer. "If one is asked to pass before the Ark ... the first time he ought to refuse, the second time he should hesitate and the third time he should stretch out his legs and go down" (34a).

There is a wonderful story told in *Pesachim* 119b, that addresses the feelings of unworthiness that cause some persons to refuse public honors.

> What is meant by, "And the child grew and was weaned [*va yiggamel*] and Abraham made a great feast on the day of Isaac's weaning [*higamel*]" (Genesis 21:8)? The Holy One, blessed be He, will make a great banquet for the righteous on the day He manifests [*yigmol*] His love to the seed of Isaac.
>
> After they have eaten and drunk, the cup of Grace will be offered to our father Abraham, that he should recite Grace, but he will answer them, "I cannot say Grace, because Ishmael issued from me."
>
> Then Isaac will be asked, "Take it and say Grace." "I cannot say Grace," he will reply, "because Esau issued from me."
>
> Then Jacob will be asked, "Take it and say Grace." "I cannot say Grace," he will reply, "because I married two sisters during [both] their lifetimes, whereas the Torah was destined to forbid them to me."
>
> Then Moses will be asked, "Take it and say Grace." "I cannot say Grace, because I was not privileged to enter the Land of Israel in life or in death."
>
> Then Joshua will be asked, "Take it and say Grace." "I cannot say Grace," he will reply, "because I was not privileged to have a son." . . .
>
> Then David will be asked, "Take it and say Grace." "I will say Grace, and it is fitting for me to say Grace," he will reply, as it is said, "I will lift up the cup of salvation and call upon the name of the Lord" (Psalms 116:13).

This midrash is occasioned by the double use of the Hebrew root *gimel-mem-lamed*, which relates to both weaning and loving care. Since it is used twice in Genesis 21:8, the rabbis assumed that one use must apply to Isaac's lifetime and the other must refer to the World to Come. There, God will give a heavenly banquet and follow the etiquette we see developed in the Talmud. God, the host, asks the guests to say grace. God proceeds according to the halachah and asks each of the greatest male guests to say the *zimmun* and Grace. Each refuses because they feel unworthy of the honor. Who ends up saying Grace? David, who is perhaps the least worthy of any of these six men to accept a public honor. If David, who committed adultery and indirectly committed murder, feels worthy to say grace at a celestial banquet, then we should not let our feelings of unworthiness prevent us from accepting the honor of praising God's name.

There is apparently a class of people who count more within a group than others: Torah scholars. These persons rank most highly on the ladder of "worth," whereas an *am ha-arets*, a Jew who does not join the chain of tradition, is the lowest (although even an *am ha-arets* apparently ranks higher on the scale than women, slaves, or children). We see this principle at work in the following *sugya*:

> **GEMARA (47a):** The disciples of Rav were once sitting and dining together when Rav Aha entered. They said, "A great man has come who can say grace for us." He said to them, "Do you think that the greatest present says the grace? One who was there from the beginning must say grace!" The law, [however], is that the greatest says grace even though he comes in at the end.

The law here affirms that how great a part one plays in the chain of tradition is more important than when one joins the group or even who is playing host or guest (although this scenario fits that paradigm as well). Rabbi Aha was a *Tanna* of the Land of Israel of the last generation of *Tannaim* (the sixth generation) and thus of an older and more venerated generation than Rav (who was a first-generation *Amora*) and certainly more venerated than Rav's pupils.

This idea that the rabbis accord more honor to those who stand in the chain of tradition than to those who do not might not seem to fit into the system of normative Jewish thought,

and with good reason. After all, the Jewish tradition emphasizes the value of every single life, regardless of how one lives
it. In *Pesachim* 25a–b, we learn that we may not kill someone
else to save our own lives. The example given there is as
follows:

> The governor of my town has ordered me, "Go and kill So-
> and-so; if not, I will kill you." Raba answered, "Let him kill you
> rather than that you should commit murder; what [reason] do
> you see [for thinking] that your blood is redder? Perhaps his
> blood is redder."

This *sugya* represents the view that we think of as a standard Jewish value: every life is precious. It doesn't matter if you
are a Talmud scholar and the person you are asked to kill is a
drug-dealing thief. You are forbidden to save your life at the
expense of his, regardless of how he lives it. How firmly one
stands in the chain of tradition does not matter: in such a situation, lives are not valued according to accomplishments but according to the intrinsic worth of every human life.

However, in this, as in almost everything else, the rabbis
are able to see two sides of the same issue. On the most basic
level of life and death, all lives are equal. But in the world of
social interaction and etiquette, the rabbis do divide people into
groups of higher and lower worth.

What lowers a person's status? Being an *am ha-arets*—literally a person of the land, but an idiom that may mean one or
both of the following: one who does not affirm the basic relationship with God through the *Shema* and its physical signs, or
one who does not join the chain of tradition.

GEMARA (47b): An *am ha-arets* is not reckoned in for *zimmun*
...Our Rabbis taught: Who is an *am ha-arets*? Anyone who does
not recite the *Shema* evening and morning. This is the view of
Rabbi Eliezer.

Rabbi Joshua says, "Anyone who does not put on *tefillin*."

Ben Azzai says, "Anyone who has not a fringe on his
garment."

Rabbi Nathan says, "Anyone who has not a mezuzah on his
door."

Rabbi Nathan bar Joseph says, "Anyone who has children and does not bring them up to the study of the Torah."

Others say, "Even if one has learnt Scripture and Mishnah, if he has not ministered to the disciples of the wise [according to Rashi—learned gemara], he is an *am ha-arets*."

Rav Huna said, "The halachah is as laid down by 'Others.'"

Today, many Jews would fall into the category *am ha-arets*. Steinsaltz (1983), in his summary of the law, states that we *do* include an *am ha-arets* in the *zimmun* so as not to make breaches within the Jewish people. However, he does state that one who has gone outside the bounds of the Jewish community is not included in the *zimmun*. To understand the effect of this etiquette in modern terms, imagine that you were eating dinner with three other people. You shared a meal with them, talked with them, and then, at the end of the meal, they decided to go to an exclusive club, which, they informed you, you could not enter. It would feel like quite a rejection to you. (Of course, women have faced this feeling for centuries.) This is not a trivial matter. It is a way of enforcing the rabbis' ideas about who counts and who does not by means of social sanctions.

What is the minimum Jewish observance that keeps us from being labeled an *am ha-arets*? For the early *Tannaim* it is affirming the basic relationship with God through the *Shema*. In their day, Jews were making the change from relating to God through sacrifices to relating to God through prayer and Torah study; thus, this is what the early *Tannaim* emphasize as the key to being Jewish. Rav Huna is an *Amora* from a much later period, and what had seemed so important to the *Tannaim* was probably already accepted in his world and could no longer be considered the "lowest common denominator" of Jewishness. In Huna's generation, it was learning gemara and helping forge new links in the chain of tradition that counted as the minimal definition of Jewishness.

However, at the root of these categories is the intensity of our core relationship with God:

GEMARA (48a): A boy [younger than 13 years old] who knows to whom the benediction is addressed (that is God) may be counted for *zimmun*. Abaye and Rava [when they were boys] were once sitting before Rabbah. Said Rabbah to them, "To whom do we address the benedictions?"

They replied, "To the All Merciful."

"And where does the All Merciful abide?" Rava pointed to the roof; Abaye went outside and pointed to the sky.

Said Rabbah to them, "Both of you will become rabbis."

And of course, both did become great rabbis. Abaye and Rava became two of the greatest teachers in Jewish history. Their greatness stemmed from their tremendous intellects, but also from their deep relationships with God.

In summary, the rabbis seem to have developed the following hierarchy of status within the Jewish world of their day:

1. Talmud scholars and their students.
2. Those who learn only Scripture and Mishnah.
3. Jewish boys who have not reached the age of majority (13 years) but who know to whom the prayer is addressed.
4. *Amei Ha-arets*.

Women and half-Jewish slaves are not included at all in this basic hierarchy.

We have now seen *who* counts in a group, but does *how many* count for anything? The following mishnah wrestles with that question.

MISHNAH (49b): How do we say *zimmun*? If there are three he [the one saying grace] says, "Let us bless [Him of whose bounty we have eaten]." If there are three plus himself he says, "Bless."

If there are ten, he says, "Let us bless our God"; if there are ten plus himself he says "Bless." It is the same whether there are ten or ten myriads [according to Rabbi Akiba].

If there are a hundred he says, "Let us bless the Lord our God"; if there are a hundred plus himself he says, "Bless."

If there are a thousand he says, "Let us bless the Lord our God, the God of Israel"; if there are a thousand plus himself he says, "Bless."

If there are ten thousand he says, "Let us bless the Lord our God, the God of Israel, the God of Hosts, who dwells among the cherubim, for the food which we have eaten." If there are ten thousand plus himself he says "Bless."

Corresponding to his invocation the others respond after him, "Blessed be the Lord our God, the God of Israel, the God of Hosts, who dwells among the cherubim, for the food which we have eaten."

Rabbi Jose the Galilean says, "The formula of invocation corresponds to the number assembled, as it says, 'Bless ye God in full assemblies, even the Lord, ye that are from the fountain of Israel'" (Psalms 68:27).

Said Rabbi Akiba, "What do we find in the synagogue? Whether there are many or few [beyond a minyan of ten, the reader] says, 'Bless ye the Lord.' Rabbi Ishmael says, 'Bless ye the Lord who is blessed.'"

GEMARA: Samuel said, "A man should never exclude himself from the general body [that is, he should always say 'Let us bless.']."

Two issues are presented in this mishnah. First, in the actual formula of the *zimmun*, does the inviter include himself in the invitation or not? And second, what impact does the number of people present make on the content of the *zimmun*? Let us take each of these questions in turn.

The rabbis decide that regardless of the number of people present, the person saying the *zimmun* should include himself in the invitation in order to include himself in the community. In so doing, he also avoids implying that he does not need to be invited to bless God's name. There is some ambivalence among the rabbis about this issue. Some of them suggest an intricate system that depends on the number of people present, summarized as follows:

10 persons including inviter (10 total); inviter says, "Let us bless."
10 persons plus the inviter (11 total); inviter says, "(You) bless."
God's name is stated as " . . . our God."

100 persons including inviter (100 total); inviter says, "Let us bless."

100 persons plus inviter (101 total); inviter says, "(You) bless."

God's name is stated as " . . . the Lord our God."

1,000 persons including inviter (1,000 total); inviter says, "Let us bless."

1,000 persons plus the inviter (1,001 total); inviter says "(You) bless."

God's name is stated as " . . . the Lord our God, the God of Israel."

10,000 persons including inviter (10,000 total); inviter says, "Let us bless."

10,000 persons plus the inviter (10,001 total); inviter says, "(You) bless."

God's name is stated as " . . . the Lord our God, the God of Israel, the God of Hosts, who dwells among the cherubim."

All these variations are rejected. The only numbers that matter are the minimum three persons needed to say *zimmun* at all, and the minimum ten persons needed to add God's name to the *zimmun*. Any number larger than ten simply does not matter. *Numbers don't count.*

This may be a difficult lesson for us to come to grips with today, particularly in organized Jewish life. So much emphasis is placed on how many people attend a service or a program, as if that were the most important measure of meaningfulness. This mishnah teaches us that we err when we use numbers as the criterion for "success" in Jewish life. *What* counts is intention and connection with God. *Who* counts are the people who experience those things.

8

The Spirituality
of the Intellect:
Who Has Authority
in Our Tradition
and Why?

T here are people who consider the intellectual to be a member of an elite. Some would say that the rabbis of the Talmud are among them. On closer examination, however, we find that the message is mixed.

Having defined our basic relationship with God in ideal and real circumstances in earlier chapters and having examined the impact that we and our desires have on this relationship, in this chapter we address the document we are reading and its validity as a way of approaching God.

While the *mishnayot* of this chapter outline the differences of opinion between Beit Hillel and Beit Shammai regarding the prayers said at meals, both the Mishnah and the Gemara examine intellectual endeavor as a part of our basic relationship with God. We know with certainty that the determination of halachah was not the main point of this chapter, for by the time the Mishnah was redacted, and all the more so by the time the Gemara was composed, the disputes between the Houses of Hillel and Shammai had long been settled.

In almost all such conflicts, the law follows the House of Hillel, as we saw in Chapter 1. The story of how Beit Hillel won this honor is one of the most beautiful in the Talmud:

"For three years there was a dispute between Beit Shammai and Beit Hillel, the former asserting, 'The law is in agreement with our views,' and the latter contending, 'The law is in agreement with our views.' Then a *bat kol* (a voice from heaven) an-

127

nounced, 'Both rulings are the words of the living God, but the law is in agreement with the rulings of Beit Hillel.'

"Since, however, 'both are the words of the living God,' what was it that entitled Beit Hillel to have the law fixed according to their rulings? Because they were kindly and modest, they studied their own rulings and those of Beit Shammai, and were even so humble as to mention the words of Beit Shammai before their own" (*Eruvin* 13b).

This story is a wonderful paradigm for conflict resolution. God must settle this dispute, so what does God do? God listens to both sides and acknowledges their validity. God then makes a decision on whose law to follow, based on the process that Beit Hillel used to come to their decisions— a process of consideration and humility. In other words, you can't separate what you think from who you are and how you behave; they are all interconnected.

However, one might ask, why did the rabbis bother including Beit Shammai's views, since we know that they're going to "lose?" Why not just transmit Hillel's view, since that is what ultimately becomes law? The *Tannaim* and *Amoraim* transmitted the views of Beit Shammai along with Beit Hillel not only because they often make valid and important points, and not only because they represented an important group within the Jewish community, but also because the very existence of the two houses and the debate they engendered are an important and valuable part of our tradition and one more pathway to God.

A modern analogy can be found in the political arena. In the 1988 race for the Democratic presidential nomination, Jesse Jackson and the "Rainbow Coalition" continued to campaign long after it became obvious that they would lose. They did so because by continuing the campaign, they raised issues of importance to them and tried to influence the general direction of the Democratic party as a whole. Beit Shammai is like such a minority group within a larger party. They might never "win," but they express their views and try to influence the decisions that are made by others.

Jacob Neusner (1973), in commenting on this chapter in his *Invitation to the Talmud*, puts it beautifully:

> The rabbis, unlike us, were able to conceive of practical and critical thinking as holy. They were able . . . to see as religiously significant, indeed as sanctified, what the modern intellectual perceives as the very instrument of secularity: the capacity to think critically and to reason. [p. xv]

In an even more subtle way, this chapter conveys who has authority in our tradition and why they have it. The opinion that ultimately holds sway may not be the "correct" one. Opinions are proposed by people whose conduct can either enhance or detract from the acceptance of their rulings. As we have noted, who we are and what we say are intimately connected in the Jewish system of thought. Beit Hillel's opinions are accepted not just because they may have been "correct," but also because they acted like *menschen*, people who respect their fellow human beings. They were committed to the holy undertaking of argumentation and did not undermine it by haughtily dismissing their opponents' opinions, as we saw in the classic text from *Eruvin* 13b. This principle regarding which opinions are accepted is demonstrated even more clearly in another famous story from *Baba Metsia* 59a–b.

> If he cut it (an oven made of many layers with sand between each layer into which an impure thing has fallen) into separate tiles, placing sand between each tile: Rabbi Eliezer declared it clean, and the Sages declared it unclean (59b); and this was the oven of Aknai. Why [the oven of] Aknai? Said Rav Judah in Samuel's name: [It means] that they encompassed it with arguments as a snake, and proved it unclean.
>
> It has been taught: On that day Rabbi Eliezer brought forward every imaginable argument, but they did not accept them. Said he to them, "If the halachah agrees with me, let this carob-tree prove it!" Thereupon the carob-tree was torn a hundred cubits out of its place—others affirm; four hundred cubits. "No proof can be brought from a carob-tree," they retorted.
>
> Again he said to them, "If the halachah agrees with me, let the stream of water prove it!" Whereupon the stream of water flowed backwards. "No proof can be brought from a stream of water," they rejoined.

Again he urged, "If the halachah agrees with me, let the walls of the school house prove it," whereupon the walls inclined to fall. But Rabbi Joshua rebuked them [the walls] saying, "When scholars are engaged in a halachic dispute, what have you to interfere?" Hence they did not fall, in honor of Rabbi Joshua, nor did they resume the upright [position] in honor of Rabbi Eliezer; and they are still standing thus inclined.

Again he said to them, "If the halachah agrees with me let it be proved from Heaven!" Whereupon a Heavenly Voice cried out, "Why do you dispute with Rabbi Eliezer, seeing that in all matters the halachah agrees with him!" But Rabbi Joshua arose and exclaimed, "It [the Torah] is not in heaven! (Deuteronomy 30:12)." What did he mean by this? Said Rabbi Jeremiah, "That the Torah had already been given at Mount Sinai; we pay no attention to a Heavenly Voice, because You have long since written in the Torah at Mount Sinai, 'After the majority one must incline' (Exodus 23:2)."

Rabbi Nathan met Elijah and asked him, "What did the Holy One, Blessed be He, do in that hour?" He laughed and replied, "My children have overcome me, my children have overcome me." It was said, "On that day all objects which Rabbi Eliezer had declared clean were brought and burnt in fire. Then they took a vote and excommunicated him. . . ."

Great was the calamity that befell that day, for everything at which Eliezer cast his eyes was burned up. Rabban Gamaliel too was traveling in a ship, when a huge wave arose to drown him. "It appears to me," he reflected, "This this is on account of none other than Rabbi Eliezer ben Hyrcanus."

Of course, there are many, many lessons that can be drawn from this story. One of them is that intellectual and spiritual gifts cannot control us: we must control them. We must never allow ourselves to become arrogant simply because we are brighter than others or have a close relationship with God. Rabbi Eliezer was a man of extraordinary spiritual and intellectual gifts. However, he could not control those gifts and did not allow God to control them. Consequently, he committed great transgressions in his anger over his excommunication. Everything upon which he looked was burned up, and he prayed for the death of his brother-in-law, Rabban Gamaliel, who had excommunicated him. His opinion about the stove's purity was undoubtedly correct, as all the supernatural signs showed, but that was not enough to have his views become law. He did not respect his colleagues, and this caused them to reject not just his ruling but him, himself.

This principle was also clearly at work in the conflict between Gamaliel and Joshua, about which we read in Chapter 4. There, Rabbi Joshua acted with more decency and ultimately won the right to determine the halachah according to his opinion. Who has authority in our tradition? The one who is committed to the process of respectful intellectual argumentation.

Only a small part of the long block of mishnah that begins this chapter will be cited here.

> **MISHNAH (51b):** These are the points [of difference] between Beit Shammai and Beit Hillel in relation to a meal. Beit Shammai say that the benediction is first said over the day and then over the wine, while Beit Hillel say that the benediction is first said over the wine and then over the day. . . .
>
> If one has eaten and forgotten to say grace, Beit Shammai say: Let him return to the place [where he ate] and say the grace, while Beit Hillel say: Let him say it in the place where he remembered. Until when can he say the grace? Until the food in his stomach is digested.

The first conflict between Beit Shammai and Beit Hillel concerns the order in which we say the Kiddush on Friday evening to begin Shabbat. Before we begin our Shabbat celebration, we say two prayers: one prayer that sanctifies the day, separating it from the rest of the week, and one prayer over the wine itself. Since the law almost always follows Beit Hillel, we say the blessing over the wine and then over the day.

This may strike us as odd. Usually we say a blessing as close as possible to the performance of the mitzvah; in other words, we would assume that we'd say the blessing over the wine and then immediately drink it rather than inserting a long blessing between the first blessing and the act. The logical order would be to say the Kiddush, the Sanctification of the Day, *then* bless the wine, then drink it.

The gemara on this section of the mishnah points out two dimensions on which the two houses base their reasoning: causality and time.

GEMARA (51b): Our Rabbis taught: The points of difference between Beit Shammai and Beit Hillel in relation to a meal are as follows:

Beit Shammai say that the blessing is first said over the [sanctity of] the day and then over the wine, because it is on account of the day that the wine is there, and [moreover] the day has already become holy before the wine has been brought.

Beit Hillel say that the blessing is said over the wine first and then over the day, because the wine provides the occasion for the benediction to be said. Another explanation is that the blessing over the wine is said frequently, while the blessing of the day is said [only] at infrequent intervals, and that which comes frequently always has precedence over that which comes infrequently.

Beit Shammai holds that the day causes the wine to be drunk. One would not drink this particular cup of wine were it not for the Shabbat. Therefore, it rules that one mentions the purpose of the wine before the actual blessing over it, almost consecrating the wine for this purpose. Beit Shammai also holds that the chronology of the Sabbath day makes it logical to say the Sanctification of the Day before the blessing over the wine. The Kiddush is said after the sun has gone down, when Shabbat has already started. Since the Sabbath day has already arrived and become holy without the benefit of the wine, one might reason that we would bless the day, since it has already begun, and then bless the wine. Beit Shammai appears to use two basic factors in coming to their decision: causality (does the day cause us to drink the wine, or does the wine cause the day to be holy? Beit Shammai holds the former; Beit Hillel, as we shall see, the latter) and chronological order (the coming of the day has preceded the bringing of the wine).

Beit Hillel uses those same dimensions to reach a different conclusion. They reason that one would not say the blessing over the day without the wine—in other words, the wine *causes* one to say the blessing—so the blessing over the wine should be said first. This is difficult to understand, since we may, in fact, say kiddush over bread when no wine is available. (In his commentary, Rashi tries to harmonize these two views by stating that the bread is merely a stand-in for the wine. A more detailed discussion of Kiddush can be found in *Pesachim* 105a–106b.)

The second reason attributed to Beit Hillel relates to time. As we have already discussed, in Jewish liturgy, things that are *tadir*—that occur with more regularity—are mentioned before those that are *sheino tadir*—that occur with less regularity. Thus, Beit Hillel reasons, wine is drunk with greater frequency than Shabbat arrives (that is, more than once a week), and so the wine should take precedence. (Interestingly, the same priority of organizational principles is seen in the structure of our tractate as a whole. Both the chronology of the day and the *tadir–sheino tadir* status are used as organizing dimensions of the tractate.)

In the second part of this portion of the mishnah, we see another characteristic dispute between the two houses. What should we do if we have eaten and forgotten to say grace? Should we return to the place where we ate? Or should we simply say grace in the place where we are when we remember that we have forgotten? Beit Shammai holds that we should return to the place where we ate, while Beit Hillel holds that we may say it where we remember that we have forgotten to say it. This difference of opinion follows the general lines of Beit Shammai's strictness and Beit Hillel's leniency.

However, Beit Shammai makes a telling point: a meal is an event sandwiched between two prayers: the grace before and after eating. In general, such events in Judaism, whether they are prayer services, Torah readings, or even the observance of Shabbat, are best fulfilled when they occur continuously, with no undue interruption or change of location until the act is completed. There is an unavoidable disruption of concentration, and a lessening of one's intention, when one interrupts an event or relocates during it. Therefore, it would seem that Beit Shammai's intuition—that in order to attain the proper intention for grace we must say it in the place where we ate—is correct. It is not ultimately practical, however. Let us say that you have a meal in the airport in Washington, D.C., before catching a plane to New York. As you are finishing your meal you hear them announce the final boarding call for your flight. You rush out of the restaurant without saying grace, and you do not remember that you forgot to say grace until you reach La Guardia Airport. The food is still sitting in your stomach (that airport food!), and returning to the place where you ate would provide you with a more sincere motivation for prayer, but returning to that restaurant is not practical. Therefore, the law allows you to say grace in New York.

While this is the minimum the law demands, it is clear that this is not the most desirable outcome. The rabbis want to strongly encourage us to maintain the integrity of the meal as a sacred moment, surrounded by prayer, as the following stories show:

> **GEMARA (53b):** "If one has eaten, etc." Rav Zebid, or some say Rav Dimi bar Abba, said, "Opinions differ only in the case where one forgot, but if he omitted it willfully everyone agrees he must return to his place and say grace." This is obvious! The Mishnah says, "has forgotten." You might think that the rule is the same even if he did it purposely, and the reason why it says "has forgotten" is to show you how stringent Beit Shammai are. Therefore we are told that this is not so.
>
> It has been taught: Beit Hillel said to Beit Shammai, "According to your words, if one ate at the top of the Temple Mount and forgot, and descended without having said grace, he should return to the top of the Temple Mount and say grace?" Beit Shammai replied to Beit Hillel, "According to your words, if one forgot a purse at the top of the Temple Mount, is he not to go up and get it? And if he will ascend for his own sake, surely he should do so all the more for the honor of Heaven!"
>
> There were once two disciples who omitted to say grace. One who did it accidentally followed the rule of Beit Shammai [and returned] and found a purse of gold, while the other who did it purposely followed the rule of Beit Hillel, and he was eaten by a lion.
>
> Rabbah bar Bar Hanah was once traveling with a caravan, and he took a meal and forgot and did not say grace. He said to himself, "What shall I do? If I say to the others, 'I have forgotten to say grace,' they will say to me, 'Say it [here]: wherever you

say the benediction you are saying it to the All-Merciful.' I had better tell them that I have forgotten a golden dove." So he said to them, "Wait for me, because I have forgotten a golden dove." He went back and said grace and found a golden dove. Why should it have been just a dove? Because the community of Israel are compared to a dove, as it is written, "The wings of the dove are covered with silver, and her pinions with the shimmer of gold" (Psalms 68:14). Just as the dove is saved only by her wings, so Israel is saved only by the mitzvot.

Clearly, the rabbis find some merit in Beit Shammai's reasoning. They cannot make Beit Shammai's views the halachah, but they can urge us, through stories such as these, to go *lifnim mishurat hadin*, beyond the letter of the law, to observe its spirit. The stories show that those who respect the integrity of a prayer event such as a meal, and return to the place where it all began in order to finish it, are not only meritorious but will be rewarded. It is interesting that Rabba bar bar Hanah, who studied in the Land of Israel for some time and saw the results of war, would encourage Israel to be like the dove who does not bite in its defense, but merely flies, rising above its troubles. So is Israel victorious when it relies on God's word and not on might. Psalm 68:12–13, which precedes the verse just cited, shows how nonviolence and reliance on God can lead to victory over armies: "The Lord gives the word: great is the company of those who bear the tidings. Kings of armies flee, they flee: and she who dwells in the house divides the spoil."

As these brief excerpts show, this chapter celebrates our intellectual ability to relate to holy texts and, through them, to God. The ability to reason through a number of opinions, to see a problem from many points of view and to analyze it from many dimensions, is shown here to be a kind of prayer. However, we must note that this is the shortest chapter in this tractate, as shown in the following table.

Several interesting phenomena can be noted in the table on p. 136. The numbers of *mishnayot* in each chapter fall within a narrow range and do not appear to correspond to the length of the Gemara chapters. (Chapter 8 of the Mishnah is one of the *longer* chapters in this tractate.) In other words, the *Amoraim* and *Saboraim*, those who shaped the Talmud, emphasized what

Tractate Berachot

Chapter	Pages	Total	Number of *Mishnayot*
1	2a–13a	22	5
2	13a–17b	10	8
3	17b–26a	17	6
4	26a–30b	9	7
5	30b–34b	8	5
6	35a–45a	20	8
7	45a–51b	13	5
8	51b–53b	5	8
9	54a–64a	21	5

seemed important to them in the Mishnah, using the Mishnah as a jumping-off point for their discussions of the themes we have outlined for each of the chapters of this tractate.

What were the *Amoraim* and *Saboraim* trying to tell us by so severely limiting their commentary to this chapter? They may have been trying to show that in the step-by-step system of relating to God that they were developing, intellect is only one means through which we can approach God, and it should not be unduly emphasized. In addition, they may have wanted to show that concentrating only on intellectual mastery of the Torah tradition is an empty exercise.

The rabbis struggled with their intellectual, elitist tendencies, as we saw in Chapter 7. Their striving to overcome those tendencies can be seen in the way they treat the intellect in this chapter. The *Amoraim* acknowledge that intellectual mastery can be very enjoyable and spiritually stimulating. However, if we use Torah study only to nourish our intellects, we may starve our souls. The rabbis wanted intellectual pursuits to be just one small part of a full relationship with God.

9

Consecrating Astonishment: How Do We Respond When We Encounter Another Dimension?

V isions and dreams. Rainbows and flowers. These are what we have come to think of as the essence of "spiritual encounters." And, indeed, they are a part of our relationship with God. In this chapter the rabbis delineate a system that helps us frame our encounters with the extraordinary. First they outline how we should respond to utterly miraculous events, such as true miracles and the prophecy we experience through our dreams. Next, they teach us how to relate to God when we encounter the marvels of nature and the wondrous variety of human form and behavior. Finally, they show us how to consecrate our appreciation of this dimension in the everyday occurrences of our lives. These topics seem to be arranged so that we start with a relatively lower level of spiritual experience and move on to higher ones.

It may seem odd that this chapter comes at the *end* of this tractate. We might have expected it to be placed at the beginning. After all, this is a tractate about *berachot*, blessings, so why does the chapter about blessings and "spiritual experiences" come last, instead of first? One might also think that the chapter's contents should be in the opposite order; do not miracles such as the parting of the Red Sea require a higher level of prayer than does the donning of one's shoes each day? No. That is precisely the point the rabbis are trying to make. Anyone can feel close to God when witnessing a miracle. Almost anyone will feel God's presence when standing on a mountaintop or looking at a rainbow. It takes a truly deep and strong relationship with God to find God in the most seemingly mundane aspects of life. To hearken back to our marriage analogy, anyone can summon up passion for a dramatic one-night stand. Almost anyone can feel infatuated for a week or so. But true love and devotion, the ability to find something special and new each day in a person we know well, can be the most difficult to maintain. The chapter, and thus the tractate, ends with a combination of these levels of love: a story of the *Shema's* daily recital in a dramatic setting.

The contents of this chapter represent the last step in the spiritual journey that the rabbis have outlined in this tractate. They began by defining our basic relationship with God; then they showed us how to overcome the things that might interfere with or destroy that relationship. Then they showed us how to incorporate our personalities into the relationship. Next, they taught us how to harness our desires to fuel that relationship. They defined who has the potential for having an especially close relationship with God. Then they explored the intellect as a way to approach God. Now, in this chapter, they finally tell us about the things many people believe prayer is about: the soaring spirit, the messages received, the encounters with dimensions of existence that do not belong to the everyday. But note that we must go through all the work outlined for us in Chapters 1 through 8 before we can truly attain this level of connection with God. This is not where prayer begins: this kind of prayer is the product of years of growth, of searching and working on our relationship with God.

A word about structure. The material in this chapter is organized in a way that plays upon our expectation that the most uniform and most frequently said (*tadir*) prayers would be placed first, as they were in the rest of the tractate. In this chapter, the usual priorities are reversed, and the most standard and *tadir* prayers are placed last, in order to bring the tractate full circle: the tractate began with the *Shema* and will end with it, too. This reversal of the priority-ordering of the material may also signal that this chapter is not so much about logic and *halachah* as it is about *aggadah*, stories that carry a moral message. There seems to be little argumentation of the law in the chapter; it is set forth without much debate. And there is much more aggadic material in this chapter than in the others. (Many tractates' final chapters have a great deal of aggadic material.)

This chapter, and thus the whole tractate, ends with a beautiful *nechemtah*, a word of comfort. In it, those who study Torah are assured that they increase peace in this world and are promised a reward in the world to come. The composition of this closing section is as deliberately thought out as the beginning of the tractate: it ends with the word *Shalom* just as so many of our prayers do, including the *Amidah*, *Birkat HaMazon*, and *Kaddish*.

We begin the chapter with the blessing over miracles:

MISHNAH (54a): If one sees a place where miracles have been wrought for Israel, he says, "Blessed . . . who wrought miracles for our fathers in this place."

GEMARA (54a): Whence is this rule [of saying a blessing over a miracle] derived? Rabbi Johanan said, "Because Scripture says, 'And Jethro said, "Blessed be the Lord who has delivered you . . ."'" (Exodus 18:10)." And is a blessing said only for a miracle wrought for many people, but not for one wrought for an individual? What of the case of the man who was traveling through Ever Yemina when a lion attacked him, but a miracle was wrought for him and he was saved? He went before Rava, who said to him, "Every time you pass that place say, 'Blessed be the One who wrought for me a miracle in this place.'" . . . .

For a miracle done for many people (that is publicly), everyone is obligated to say a blessing. For a miracle wrought for an individual, that individual (alone) is obligated to say a blessing.

The mishnah begins with the most obvious case of what we might say a blessing over: a miracle. Nothing could make us feel more quickly and obviously in contact with God's essence than experiencing a suspension of the laws of nature performed for our benefit. In addition, this first blessing frames the content of the entire chapter. What is a blessing? It is the consecration of memories, one of the hallmarks of Judaism. This is clearly brought out in the gemara.

We do not say blessings as a *pro forma* exercise, as if racking up points in a numbers game; the purpose is not to see how many we can say in one day. Rather, we say them, as we saw in Chapter 6, to consecrate our deepest emotions and drives. Therefore, we do not say a blessing over the place where a miracle was wrought for another individual. We would have no memory, no feeling of gratitude, to be consecrated. However, when the miracle happened to a large group, and the story becomes part of the collective history of the group, then we say a blessing over the memory regardless of whether the miracle happened to us personally or the memory of it comes from belonging to the group who experienced it.

It is interesting that Rabbi Johanan cites Jethro, a non-Jew, as the source of this blessing. He uttered this blessing when Moses, his son-in-law, told him of all the miracles God had wrought for the Jewish people on their way out of Egypt. Thus, the first blessing over miracles wrought for a group in the Torah is uttered by a non-Jew.

The urge to remember and give thanks is probably universal. Think of the place where something wonderful happened to you: you saw a deer, your child was born, you learned something wonderful. Now imagine returning to the place where this event happened. You would probably want to consecrate your feelings of gratitude and wonder as you recalled that moment. That is what this blessing is for.

One of the most miraculous events we could experience is direct communication from God. Such prophecy is no longer given to us. However, we may still receive one-sixtieth of prophecy in our dreams.

> **GEMARA (57b):** Five things are a sixtieth part [of something else]: namely fire, honey, and Sabbath, and sleep and a dream. Fire is one-sixtieth part of Gehinnom. Honey is one-sixtieth part of manna. Sabbath is one-sixtieth part of the world to come. Sleep is one-sixtieth a part of death. A dream is one-sixtieth part of prophecy.

We are given only tastes of the other dimensions that exist beyond our consciousness. However, even if all we do is fill our lives with one-sixtieth of the intensity of these realms, we will have enriched ourselves. Note the symmetry in these "five things." Fire is one-sixtieth of *Gehinnom*, and Shabbat is its opposite, one-sixtieth of the World to Come. Of course, we are prohibited from kindling fire on Shabbat, forbidden to mix the tastes we are given of these two different realms beyond life. On the other hand, to receive a small taste of prophecy through a dream, we must enter a small part of death, sleep. We have seen this correlation between risking death and being close to God before, in Chapter 3.

This chapter contains a lengthy section on dreams. Why is this subject covered here? This material is included at this point because dreams are a way in which God contacts us, now that direct communication with God—prophecy—has ceased in Israel. Like Jacob in the Torah, with whom God communicated mostly through dreams, we tend to have our guard up. Like Jacob, we are often looking out for our best interests, trying to control our lives. It is difficult for God's messages to enter our consciousnesses while we hold this attitude. Therefore, God reaches out to us when we are more open, less defended—in sleep.

Dreams as a form of Divine communication, and instrument of Divine justice, are featured in the following story of Bar Hadaya, the dream interpreter. It is a fable about the dire consequences of misusing our spiritual gifts to serve our greed.

GEMARA (56a): Bar Hadaya was an interpreter of dreams. To one who paid him he used to give a favorable interpretation and to one who did not pay him he gave an unfavorable interpretation.

Abaye and Rava each had a dream. Abaye gave him a zuz, and Rava did not give him anything. They said to him, "In our dream we had to read the verse, 'Your ox shall be slain before your eyes' (Deuteronomy 28:31)." To Rava he said, "Your business will be a failure, and you will be so grieved that you will have no appetite to eat." To Abaye he said, "Your business will prosper, and you will not be able to eat from sheer joy."

They then said to him, "We had to read in our dream the verse, 'You shall beget sons and daughters but they shall not be yours' (Deuteronomy 28:41)." To Rava he interpreted it in its [literal] unfavorable sense. To Abaye he said, "You have numerous sons and daughters, and your daughters will be married and go away, and it will seem to you as if they have gone into captivity."

[They said to him:] "We were made to read the verse, 'Your sons and your daughters shall be given unto another people' (Deuteronomy 28:32)." To Abaye he said, "You have numerous sons and daughters; you will want your daughters to marry your relatives, and your wife will want them to marry her relatives, and she will force you to marry them to her relatives, which will be like giving them to another people." To Rava he said, "Your wife will die, and her sons and daughters will come under the sway of another wife." . . .

[They further said:] "We were made to read in our dream the verse, 'Go your way, eat your bread with joy' (Ecclesiastes 9:7)." To Abaye he said, "Your business will prosper, and you will eat and drink, and recite this verse out of the joy of your heart." To Rava he said, "Your business will fail, you will slaughter [cattle] and not eat or drink and you will read Scripture to allay your anxiety."

[They said to him:] "We were made to read the verse, 'You shall carry much seed out into the field, [and shall gather little in, for the locusts will consume it]' (Deuteronomy 28:38)." To Abaye he interpreted from the first half of the verse; to Rava from the second half.

[They said to him:] "We were made to read the verse, 'You shall have olive trees throughout all your borders, [but you shall not anoint yourself with oil]' (Deuteronomy 38:49)." To Abaye he interpreted from the first half of the verse; to Rava from the second half.

[They said to him:] "We were made to read the verse, 'And all the peoples of the earth shall see that the name of the Lord is called upon you, and they shall be afraid of you' (Deuteronomy 28:10)." To Abaye he said, "Your name will become famous as head of the college, and you will be generally feared." To Rava he said, "The King's treasury will be broken into, and you will be arrested as a thief, and everyone will draw an inference from you." [The Soncino translation notes this is the treasury where the tax payments were received.] The next day the King's treasury was broken into and they came and arrested Rava.

They said to him, "We saw a lettuce on the mouth of a jar." To Abaye he said, "Your business will be doubled like a lettuce." To Rava he said, "Your business will be bitter like a lettuce."

They said to him, "We saw some meat on the mouth of a jar." To Abaye he said, "Your wine will be sweet, and everyone will come to buy meat and wine from you." To Rava he said, "Your wine will turn sour, and everyone will come to buy meat to eat with it." [The Soncino translation notes: to dip in it.]

They said to him, "We saw a cask hanging on a palm tree." To Abaye he said, "Your business will spring up like a palm tree." To Rava he said, "Your goods will be sweet like dates." [Rashi: sweeter to the customer because of their cheapness].

They said to him, "We saw a pomegranate sprouting on the mouth of a jar." To Abaye he said, "Your goods will be high-priced like a pomegranate." To Rava he said, "Your goods will be stale like a [dry] pomegranate."

They said to him, "We saw a cask fall into a pit." To Abaye he said, "Your goods will be in demand according to the saying, 'The *pu'ah* (a dyer's vegetable madder, a prophylactic) has fallen into a well and cannot be found.'" To Rava he said, "Your goods will be spoiled and they will be thrown into a pit."

They said to him, "We saw a young ass standing by our pillow and braying." To Abaye he said, "You will become a king, and an Amora [an interpreter] will stand by you." To Rava he said, "The words 'The first-born of an ass' (Exodus 13:13) have been erased from your *tefillin*." Rava said to him, "I have looked at them and they are there." He replied to him, "Certainly the *vav* (a Hebrew letter) of the word *hamor* (ass) has been erased from your *tefillin*."

Subsequently Rava went to him by himself and said to him, "I dreamt that the outer door fell." He said, "Your wife will die." He said to him, "I dreamt that my front and back teeth fell out." He said to him, "Your sons and your daughters will die."

He said to him, "I saw two pigeons flying." He replied, "You will divorce two wives."

He said to him, "I saw two turnip-tops." He replied, "You will receive two blows with a cudgel." On that day Rava went and sat all day in the *Beit HaMidrash*. He found two blind men quarreling with one another. Rava went to separate them and they gave him two blows. They wanted to give him another blow but he said, "Enough! I saw in my dream only two."

Finally Rava went and gave him a fee. He said to him, "I saw a wall fall down." He replied, "You will acquire wealth without end."

He said, "I dreamt that Abaye's villa fell in and the dust of it covered me." He replied to him, "Abaye will die and [the presidency of] his College will be offered to you."

He said to him, "I saw my own villa fall in, and everyone came and took a brick." He said to him, "Your teachings will be disseminated throughout the world."

He said to him, "I dreamt that my head was split open and my brains fell out." He replied, "The stuffing will fall out of your pillow."

He said to him, "In my dream I was made to read the Hallel of Egypt." He replied, "Miracles will happen to you."

Bar Hadaya was once traveling with Rava in a boat. He said to himself, "Why should I accompany a man to whom a miracle will happen?" As he was disembarking, he let fall a book. Rava found it, and saw written in it, "All dreams follow the mouth." He exclaimed, "Wretch! It all depended on you and you gave me all this pain! I forgive you everything except [what you said about] the daughter of Rabbi Hisda (his wife). May it be God's will that this fellow be delivered up to the Government, and that they have no mercy on him!"

Bar Hadaya said to himself, "What am I to do? We have been taught that a curse uttered by a sage, even when undeserved, comes to pass; how much more this of Rava, which was deserved!" He said, "I will rise up and go into exile. For a Master has said, 'Exile makes atonement for iniquity.'" He rose and fled to the Romans.

He went and sat at the door of the keeper of the King's wardrobe. The keeper of the wardrobe had a dream, and said to him, "I dreamt that a needle pierced my finger." He said to him, "Give me a *zuz*!" He refused to give him one, and would not say a word to him.

He again said to him, "I dreamt that a worm fell between two of my fingers." He said to him, "Give me a *zuz*." He refused to give him one, and he would not say a word to him.

"I dreamt that a worm filled the whole of my hand." He said to him, "Worms have been spoiling all of the silk garments." This became known in the palace and they brought the keeper of the wardrobe in order to put him to death. He said to them, "Why execute me? Bring the man who knew and would not tell."

So they brought Bar Hadaya, and they said to him, "Because of your *zuz*, the king's silken garments have been ruined (56b). They tied two cedars together with a rope, tied one leg to one cedar and the other to the other, and released the rope, so that even his head was split. Each tree rebounded to its place and he was decapitated and his body fell in two.

The key to the meaning of this whole story is in the name *Bar Hadaya*. Its *shoresh*—its root letters—are *dalet-aleph-hay*, and it occurs only five times in the entire *Tanach*. In Leviticus 11:14, it is used as a noun, to describe an unclean bird. Three times it is used as a verb, to describe the actions of an enemy who will swoop down on its victim like an eagle, suddenly and with no warning (Deuteronomy 28:49, Jeremiah 48:40, and Jeremiah 49:22). Note that the Deuteronomy passage is part of the long series of curses (Deuteronomy 27:11–28:69) that is featured extensively in the *sugya* itself. The final instance of this *shoresh*, *dalet-aleph-hay* is in Psalm 18:11. There the verb describes God "soaring on the wings of the wind." (Significantly, the word *wind*, *ruach*, can also mean "the spirit.") Thus, when this *shoresh* refers to animals or people, it is as an instrument of parasitic destruction. When it refers to an action of God's, it is the most beautiful and elevating motion. This dichotomy expresses the point of this story: when spiritual gifts are used in God's service, they elevate us in the most beautiful way. When they are directed toward earthly power or gain, they are destructive and unclean.

This idea is borne out in the Aramaic use of this *shoresh*. According to Jastrow's *Aramaic Dictionary* (1903) when the letters of Bar Hadaya's name are vocalized *Hedya*, it means "presence, directness"—a positive quality. However, when his name is vocalized *Hadaya*, as it is by both Jastrow and Steinsaltz (1983), it refers to an unclean bird of the hawk species (Jastrow, p.333). This is an even clearer indication of the different meanings this *shoresh* can have. Bar Hadaya, using his gifts to increase his wealth, is like an unclean bird of prey. He soars, but only to dive, kill, and eventually be killed. Had he merited the name *Bar Hedya*, he would have used his insight into dreams to bring himself closer to God.

One more word about personalities: there may be some melding of the personalities of Rava, the Babylonian *Amora* who died in 352 C.E. and who was Abaye's contemporary, and Rabba bar Nachmani (260–340). Rava was married to the daughter of his teacher, Hisda. However, according to the *Encyclopedia Judaica* (1972, vol. 13, p. 1579), Rava was quite wealthy and maintained close ties with the secular authorities, making it unlikely that he would be arrested for raiding the treasury. It also seems unlikely that Bar Hadaya's forecasts of economic doom either came true or would bother him, given his secure economic status. Rabbah bar Nachmani, on the other hand, was quite poor and so would have taken Bar Hadaya's predictions to heart. Rabbah was a very popular teacher but was also intensely disliked by the members of his community, whom he frequently denounced. They did not support him when he was accused of urging the large audiences that came to hear him to avoid paying a poll tax. It was on this account that authorities were sent to seize him and he was forced to flee. He wandered about Pumbedita, and his corpse was found in a thicket there. Both Rabbah bar Nachmani and Rava had ties to Abaye: the former was his teacher and uncle; the latter, his colleague. Thus, either Rabbah or Rava could have gone with Abaye to consult with Bar Hadaya.

Dream interpretation, whether performed by Bar Hadaya or by Joseph in the Torah, seems to be both spiritually and physically risky. Both Bar Hadaya and Joseph used their special insight into dreams, and their special relationship with God, for their own gain, and both were punished for it with premature deaths in exile. We learn in Exodus 1:6 that Joseph died before his brothers. The Gemara states that this was Joseph's punishment for assuming airs of authority (55a). Bar Hadaya also died prematurely in exile, as seen in our *sugya*. In other words, when we make use of our spiritual gifts for our own personal gain, it causes our death.

Now let us turn to the story itself. This is an exceptionally long story. Therefore, we must assume that the story's length conveys some message. As we analyze it, we see that Rava and Abaye first bring seven dreams to Bar Hadaya in which each man dreamed of the identical Torah verse (a *highly* unlikely series of coincidences). Four of these verses, Deuteronomy 28:31, 32, 38, and 40, come from the section in the Torah that is a long series of curses. Nonetheless, Bar Hadaya finds a way to interpret them for the good for Abaye and for the bad for Rava. Note that although the cause is fortunate for Abaye and sad for Rava, the *outcome* in at least the first two cases is the same. Finally, after the seventh dream is interpreted, Bar Hadaya's prediction comes true.

In the next section, Rava and Abaye bring six dreams containing identical symbols to Bar Hadaya for interpretation. Note that the pessimistic interpretations given to Rava in this section are all economic in nature, save for the last one. These would have been more of a blow to Rabbah bar Nachmani than to Rava. After the sixth dream, Bar Hadaya's prediction is fulfilled: a letter had been erased from Rava's *tefillin*.

Finally, Rava approaches Bar Hadaya by himself and reports four dreams to him. After the fourth exchange, Bar Hadaya's prediction comes true: Rava is beaten by two blind men. It is clear that Rava finally believes in Bar Hadaya's predictive powers. Now Rava pays Bar Hadaya, and favorable predictions are wrought from the most gruesome dreams. Although we do not see a miracle worked for Rava immediately, we do see Bar Hadaya, cursed by Rava, suffering from that curse.

Here we see the true point of the story. Greed causes suffering. However, repentance, *teshuvah*, can overcome curses we bring on ourselves through avarice. Rava suffered because he did not pay Bar Hadaya. Once he did *teshuvah* and paid him, his fortunes were reversed. And even though Bar Hadaya has shown himself to be thoroughly corrupt in the use of his spiritual gifts, he is still given two chances to repent before the curse against him is fulfilled. Twice the king's steward asks him to interpret his dreams, and twice he refuses. He gives an interpretation for the third dream, but by then it is too late. The die is cast.

Note that the rabbis condemn greed, not making a living. They censure Bar Hadaya's change in the conduct of his work because of money, but they do not begrudge him an income from it. As it is said in *Pirkei Avot* 3:21, "where there is no bread, there is no Torah." Rabban Gamaliel makes a similar point in *Pirkei Avot* 2:2: "It is well to combine Torah study with some *derech erets* [here, translated as worldly occupation], for the two of them tire one out and keep sin from the mind. And all Torah that is not accompanied by work will in the end be vain and cause sin. Let all those who work with the public work with them out of a fear of God." In other words, Rabban Gamaliel knew that when we approach religious duties as our living, without any spirit of volunteerism, we are in danger of losing the very meaning of our work. We become Bar Hadayas instead of Bar Hedyas—birds of prey that search the skies rather than spirits who can soar even higher.

There is no doubt that there are persons who have a talent, if we can use such a word, for relating to God. They are blessed with a gift, but they have to use that gift correctly to fulfill their promise. It is not enough to follow spiritual leaders because they have this "talent." If they do not use this gift correctly, they can be worse than someone who does not possess this gift at all.

Could the rabbis really have believed that a dream interpreter could make a great sage suffer? And could the rabbis have believed that an *Amora*, even one as great as Rava, could bring death upon another human being through a curse if it was not part of God's plan? This hardly seems consistent with the rabbinic point of view—that even though free will is given to us, God controls our lives (*Avot* 3:19). In light of this, it is doubtful that Rava blamed Bar Hadaya for his pain. More likely, Rava and Abaye were testing Bar Hadaya with these contrived identical dreams to show him the immorality of his ways. One might even say that, formally, it was only Rava who tested him by not paying the *zuz*.

Rava entrapped Bar Hadaya, and his hubris in testing a fellow human being, setting himself up as Judge, hurt him as well as Bar Hadaya. First Rava was hurt by the civil authorities after seven tests of Bar Hadaya. Then he was hurt religiously after six tests, but still he did not stop. Finally, he was hurt physically after only four tests. At last, Rava understood: he may have been trying to force Bar Hadaya to see the error of his ways and do *teshuvah*, but he, too, erred by taking on airs of authority. The stakes kept rising as Rava's punishments became ever more basic and occurred in ever quicker succession.

God gives us chances to learn our lessons less painfully before we have to suffer to learn them. In this story, as in our own lives, the person who acted like the greatest *mensch* suffered the least; the one who acted with the least *menschlichkeit* suffered the most. Abaye, who acted the most decently, did not suffer at all in this story. Rava, who acted with less *menschlichkeit*, suffered more. Bar Hadaya, who acted in the worst manner, suffered the most. This story is a cautionary tale that warns of the consequences of misusing our spiritual gifts.

The mishnah now goes on to deal with the next level of prayer: blessing God for the extraordinary in nature and in the normal course of our lives.

> **MISHNAH (54a):** For shooting stars and for earthquakes and for thunderclaps and for storms and for lightning one says, "Blessed be the One whose strength and might fill the world."
>
> For mountains and for hills, and for seas and for rivers and for deserts one says, "Blessed be the One who made creation."
>
> Rabbi Judah says, "One who sees the Great Sea says, 'Blessed be the One who made the Great Sea.'" [That is] if he sees it at [considerable] intervals.
>
> For rain and for good tidings one says, "Blessed be the One who is good and bestows good."
>
> For evil tidings one says, "Blessed be the One, the True Judge."
>
> One who built a new house and one who bought new vessels says, "Blessed be the One who has kept us alive and preserved us and brought us to this season."
>
> One says a blessing for evil, similar to that said over good [tidings] and over good a blessing is said similar to that over evil. And one who cries over something that is past; behold he [utters] a vain prayer. If a man's wife is pregnant and he says, "[God] grant that my wife bear a male child," this is a vain prayer. If he is coming on the way and heard a voice crying in the city, and says, "[God] grant that this is not in my house," this is a vain prayer. . . .

Anyone who has seen the glories of the Rocky Mountains or the splendor of the night sky over the Red Sea knows how small a person can feel when viewing the vastness of creation. Such a state of awe might render us speechless. Therefore, the Jewish tradition gives us words with which to frame our feelings within the context of our relationship with God.

Our feelings can be overwhelming when bad fortune befalls us as well. Our tradition affirms that good and bad alike come from God. There is no room for a belief in two gods, a god of good and a god of evil. This belief, called Gnosticism, was one of the ideas against which the rabbis battled most vigorously. These days, many of us may be tempted to practice a modified form of Gnosticism. We may try to give God credit for the good things that happen to us and then blame any ill fortune we suffer on fate, chance, or luck. This is not the Jewish way. The one God is the author of our destiny.

One blessing in the foregoing mishnah should be familiar : the *Shehechiyanu*. In the mishnah, we are instructed to say this prayer when we acquire some new object. As they often do, the *Amoraim* add to, and change, the application of this *berachah* to make it reflect their values.

> **GEMARA (58b):** Rabbi Joshua ben Levi said, "One who sees a friend after a lapse of thirty days says, 'Blessed be the One who has kept us alive and preserved us and brought us to this season.'"

In this case, the *Amoraim* deemphasize possessions and lay more stress on consecrating relationships. We frequently see this tendency of the Gemara to transform the physical, material ideas of the Mishnah into the terms of relationships. For example, in the first chapter of the tractate *Baba Batra*, the Mishnah defines what it means to belong to a community on the physical plane: one has certain obligations to contribute to the repair of walls, the building of gate houses and so on. The *Amoraim* extend this concept of "belonging to a community" beyond the physical level to the interpersonal level. They define membership in a community as obligations to ransom captives, feed the hungry, cloth the naked, and the like. In other words, belonging to a community entails an obligation to maintain relationships between people, not just an obligation to maintain physical structures.

The blessing the mishnah mandates for evil tidings, "Blessed be the True Judge," may seem cruel, yet it is actually helpful. When a loved one dies, and we cut our garments as a sign of mourning and say this blessing, we are not saying that God is just per se—a declaration that would be almost impossible to make in a state of deep bereavement. Rather, it is an affirmation: "This is the truth. This person is dead. I trust that I will understand God's justice in time." It is helpful to have these words of acceptance to say at that moment of death when the natural, but unhealthy, tendency is to deny the reality of the situation.

This acceptance of reality is the first step toward dealing with, and so appreciating, anything in this world. The following *sugya* demonstrates how we can even consecrate misfortune once we have accepted it and its source, God.

GEMARA (58b): Rabbi Joshua ben Levi said, "On seeing pock-marked persons one says, 'Blessed be He who makes various creatures.'" An objection was raised: If one sees a negro, a very red or very white person, a hunchback, a dwarf or a dropsical person, he says, "Blessed be He who makes various creatures." If he sees one with an amputated limb, or blind, or flatheaded, or lame, or smitten with boils, or pock-marked, he says, "Blessed be the True Judge!" There is no contradiction: one blessing is said if he is so from birth, the other if he became so afterwards. A proof of this is that he is placed in the same category as one with an amputated limb. This proves it.

Every feeling, every experience can fuel the relationship with God—even pity or fear. First we must identify it and accept it, and then we can begin to appreciate the holiness in what we see. In essence, there are two different prayers we can say when we see someone or something that is strange or frightening to us. If the person has been as he or she is since birth, then we praise God for the variety of beings on the earth. If the person has suffered a misfortune, then we say a different blessing, praising God's judgment. Both prayers try to help us empathize with the person before us. When faced with some-

one who is handicapped or of a different race or who has suffered some misfortune, we may have a tendency to separate
ourselves from that person. We may want to say, "He is different from me, and so I am not deeply connected to him." The
berachot help us remember that this is not, and can never be,
the case. We are all connected to one another.

Of course, one could also interpret this *sugya* as represent-
ing inherent bigotry in the rabbinic mind. The rabbis evidently
struggled with those feelings. On the one hand, they felt that
to be a free, Jewish, grown man engaged in the study of Torah
was the finest form of human existence (see the commentary
on *Menachot* 43b). On the other hand, it is the rabbis who
wrote:

> **MISHNAH, Sanhedrin** (37a): Furthermore, [Adam was cre-
> ated alone] for the sake of peace among men, that one might not
> say to his fellow, "My father was greater than thine" ... [And]
> to proclaim the greatness of the Holy One, Blessed be He: for if a
> man strikes many coins from one mould, they all resemble one
> another, but the Supreme King of Kings, the Holy One blessed
> be He, fashioned every man in the stamp of the first man, and
> yet not one of them resembles his fellow. Therefore every single
> person is obliged to say: the world was created for my sake.

The rabbis made a distinction between prayers, like those
in the last *sugya*, that consecrate deep emotions, thereby facilitating the acceptance of those emotions, and prayers that are
an inappropriate plea to God to change a fate we do not want
to accept. The rabbis ruled that we do not pray about things
that cannot be changed, such as the fate of a fetus during various phases of pregnancy.

> **GEMARA (60a):** "If a man's wife is pregnant and he says,
> 'May [God] grant that my wife bear, etc.' this is a vain
> prayer. ..." During the first three days a person should ask for
> mercy, that the seed should not putrefy. From the third to the
> fortieth day he should ask for mercy that the child should be a
> male; from the fortieth day to three months he should ask for
> mercy that it not be a *sandal* (i.e., a miscarriage); from three
> months to six months he should ask for mercy that it should not

be still-born; from six months to nine months he should ask for mercy that it will come out [of the womb] in peace.

But does such a prayer avail? Has not Rav Isaac the son of Rav Ammi said, "If the man first emits seed, the child will be a girl; if the woman first emits seed, the child will be a boy?...With what case are we dealing here? If, for instance, they both emitted seed at the same time.

Some of the rabbis obviously thought that the gender of a fetus was determined around 40 days into a pregnancy, while others, represented by Rav Isaac bar Ammi, suspected that the baby's gender was determined at conception. From examining abortuses, the rabbis were able to determine the gender of aborted fetuses that they examined only after approximately 40 gestational days. Yet the rabbis had an intuition that the matter had been determined long before. In this *sugya*, they struggle to reconcile these two views.

The rabbis believed that the gender of the child was determined by who "emitted seed" (that is, reached orgasm) first. If the woman did, the child would be a boy; if the man did, the child would be a girl. They therefore reconcile this "knowledge" and this *sugya* by allowing such prayers only when the pregnancy began with a simultaneous orgasm and the outcome was thus, in their minds, not yet determined. Using this logic, the rabbis hold fast to their basic principle: we may not pray over something that is already irrevocably determined. Such prayers are not worthy of the name.

The final third of this chapter shows us how to find God's presence in our everyday lives. We began this chapter by examining miracles—a clear case of contact with the extraordinary. Next we moved on to events and feelings through which we can feel that extra dimension in events that are not miraculous, such as rainbows, lightning, and mountains. Now the rabbis examine blessings for everyday miracles, *Birkot HaShachar*, the benedictions for the morning. In other words, the most difficult spiritual task is finding the marvelous in the mundane.

GEMARA (60b): When he hears the cock crowing he should say, "Blessed be the One who has given the cock the understanding to distinguish between day and night."

When he opens his eyes he should say, "Blessed be the One who opens the eyes of the blind."

When he stretches himself and sits up, he should say, "Blessed be the One who loosens the bound."

When he dresses he should say, "Blessed be the One who clothes the naked."

When he draws himself up he should say, "Blessed be the One who raises the bowed."

When he steps on to the ground he should say, "Blessed be the One who spread the earth on the waters."

When he commences to walk he should say, "Blessed be the One who makes firm the steps of man."

When he ties his shoes he should say, "Blessed be the One who has supplied all my wants."

When he fastens his girdle, he should say, "Blessed be the One who girds Israel with might."

When he spreads a kerchief over his head he should say, "Blessed be the One who crowns Israel with glory."

In a marriage, it may be difficult to recapture the wonder of new love every day. So, too, in our relationship with God, it takes effort on our part to remember to feel thankful for the miracles we experience daily. The essence of romance is keeping love fresh, in our marriages *and* in our relationship with God. The blessings just outlined are designed to help us become aware of God's bounty as we awake and start our day.

Note that the blessings that many find offensive (those thanking God for "not making me a woman," for "not making me a non-Jew," and for "not making me a slave") do not come from this tractate of the Talmud. They are taken from tractate *Menachot*, 43b. There, the text states that we must say one hundred blessings daily and that these three must be among them. These three blessings reflect the rabbis' attitude that we saw in the *sugya* from 58b. For them, the ideal form of existence was to be a free, Jewish, grown man engaged in the study of Torah. However, it is interesting that the redactors of this tractate did not feel that these three blessings belonged in the group of blessings with which we begin each day.

Part of appreciating the wonder within our everyday lives depends on learning to trust God.

GEMARA (60b): Rav Huna said in the name of Rav citing Rabbi Meir, and so it was taught in the name of Rabbi Akiba: A man should always accustom himself to say, "Whatever the All-Merciful does is for good," [as exemplified in] the following incident. Rabbi Akiba was once going along the road and he came to a certain town and looked for lodgings but was everywhere refused. He said, "Whatever the All-Merciful does is for good," and he went and spent the night in the open field. He had with him a cock, an ass, and a lamp. A gust of wind came and blew out the lamp, a weasel came and ate the cock, and a lion came and ate the ass. He said, "Whatever the All-Merciful does is for good." The same night some brigands came and carried off the inhabitants of the town. He said to them, "Did I not say to you, 'Whatever the All-Merciful does (61a) is all for good?'"

How could Rabbi Akiba praise God's goodness when he could not find lodgings, his lamp blew out, and his ass and cock were killed? Because he had an intense trust in God. Had he been in the town, he would have been captured. Had his lamp not been blown out, the robbers might have seen him, and had his animals not been killed, they might have drawn attention to Rabbi Akiba and so put him at risk. Rabbi Akiba was quite advanced along his path of spiritual growth, as we saw in Chapter 3. He alone, of the four who entered "paradise"—that is, mystical speculation—was unharmed. He was able to brave danger because of his trust in God.

Now we start to come full circle. We began the tractate with the *Shema*, the affirmation of our most basic relationship with God. Now we will see how the most extraordinary part of that relationship can be expressed as well.

GEMARA (61b): Our Rabbis taught: Once the wicked Government [Rome] issued a decree forbidding Israel to occupy themselves with the Torah. Pappus ben Judah came and found Rabbi Akiba publicly bringing gatherings together and occupying himself with the Torah. He said to him, "Akiba, are you not afraid of the Government?" He replied, "I will explain to you with a parable. To what is this [situation] similar? A fox was once walking alongside of a river, and he saw fishes going in schools from one place to another. He said to them, 'From what are you fleeing?' They replied, 'From the nets cast for us by people.' He said to them, 'Would you like to come up on to the dry land so that you and I can live together in the way that my ancestors lived with your ancestors?' They replied, 'Are you the one that they call the cleverest of animals? You are not clever; rather, you are foolish. If we are afraid in the element in which we live, how much more in the element in which we would die!'

"So it is with us. If such is our condition when we sit and study the Torah, of which it is written, 'For it is your life and the length of your days' (Deuteronomy 30:20), if we go and neglect it how much worse off we would be!"

They said, it was only a few days until Rabbi Akiba was arrested and thrown into prison, and Pappus ben Judah was also arrested and imprisoned next to him. He said to him, "Pappus, who brought you here?" He replied, "Happy are you, Rabbi Akiba, that you have been seized for busying yourself with the Torah! Alas for Pappus, who has been seized for busying himself with idle things!"

When they took Rabbi Akiba out for execution, it was the hour for the recital of the Shema. And while they combed his flesh with iron combs, he was accepting upon himself the kingship of heaven [i.e., saying the first part of the Shema]. His students said to him, "Our teacher, even to this point?" He said to them, "All my days I have been troubled by this verse, 'with all your soul,' [which I interpret] even if He takes thy soul. I said, 'When shall I have the opportunity of fulfilling this?' Now that I have the opportunity shall I not fulfill it?"

He prolonged the word *echad* [one] until he expired while saying it. A *Bat Kol* went forth and proclaimed, "Happy are you, Akiba, that your soul has departed with the word *echad*!" The ministering angels said before the Holy One, blessed be He, "Is this Torah, and is this its reward?" [He should have been] "from them that die by Your hand, O Lord" (Psalms 17:14). He replied to them, "Their portion is in life" (Psalms 17:14).

A *Bat Kol* went forth and proclaimed, "Happy are you, Rabbi Akiba, that you are destined for the life of the world to come."

Rabbi Akiba was persecuted during the rule of Publius Aelius Hadrian, the Roman emperor from 117 to 138 C.E. Hadrian decided to erect a Roman city on the ruins of Jerusalem and call it Aelia Capitolina, in honor of himself. This may have been one of the causes of the Bar Kokhba Revolt, which lasted from 132 to 135, and in which Rabbi Akiba was involved. After his general, Julius Severus, crushed the revolt, Hadrian issued harsh decrees restricting Jewish activities. He made circumcision and Torah study capital offenses. After the revolt, Hadrian built a temple to Jupiter where the Temple had stood. Hadrian's decrees were not reversed until his son took the reins of power.

Rabbi Akiba was executed by the Hadrianic government and became the model of Jewish martyrdom. Not only did he brave death to teach Torah, but he suffered death gladly, happy that he could genuinely fulfill yet another *mitzvah* with his dying breath. To this day some Jews stretch out the last word of the *Shema*, in part as a recollection of Rabbi Akiba's faith.

In *Sefer Zichron Shalom*, a commentary on *Berachot*, it is noted that Rabbi Akiba was saying the first line of the *Shema*, which is called the Yoke of the Kingship of Heaven. In Hebrew it is called *Ol Malchut Shamayim*. The first letters of these words, when rearranged, spell *Shema*. In other words, the acceptance of God's rule in our lives is the core of the *Shema*'s message. To be able to fulfill the complete meaning of the *Shema* with all his heart and soul and body was a supreme joy to Akiba. The version of this story in the Jerusalem Talmud reports that Rabbi Akiba laughed with joy as he fulfilled this *mitzvah*.

Rabbi Akiba's acceptance of God's will in his life is summed up by Bar Kappara:

> **GEMARA (63a):** Bar Kappara expounded, "What short text is there upon which all the essential principles of the Torah depend? 'In all your ways acknowledge Him and He will direct your paths' (Proverbs 3:6)."

This is the final message of this tractate of the Gemara. Once we have made the long spiritual journey it has outlined, all that is left is to give up control over the journey to God. It is ironic that one has to *gain* control in order to give it up. But that is the ultimate goal of the journey: to be so in touch with God's presence that we need not strive to reach for it anymore. It is there, guiding us in everything we do. Having achieved that, all that is left is a word of comfort and farewell, and a reassurance of the reward that awaits us at the journey's end.

> **GEMARA (64a):** "Great peace have they that love Your law, and there is no stumbling for them (Psalms 119:165)." "Peace be within your walls and prosperity within your palaces (Psalms 122:7)." "For my brethren and companions' sake I will now say, 'Peace be within you' (Psalms 122:8)." "For the sake of the house of the Lord our God I will seek your good (Psalms 122:9)." "The Lord will give strength unto His people, the Lord will bless His people with peace (Psalms 29:11)."

Appendix I: The Sages

The following summaries are taken from Mielziner's *Introduction to the Talmud* (1968), Steinsaltz's *Reference Guide to the Talmud* (1989), his Hebrew commentary on this tractate (1983), the *Encyclopedia Judaica* (1973), The *El Am Talmud Commentary* (1982), and Hyman's (1910) *Toldot Tannaim v'Amoraim*.

Abaye was a fourth-generation Babylonian *Amora* (280–338). He was esteemed for his dialectical abilities, as well as his integrity and gentleness. He was a contemporary of Rava (299–352), and the two held many discussions, but Rava's opinion prevailed in all but six cases.

Abba Saul was a mid–second century *Tanna*, probably a disciple of Rabbi Akiba, for Abba Saul quotes several *halachot* in Akiba's name. He is not usually mentioned with other *Tannaim*, nor are *halachot* transmitted in his name by later *Tannaim*. He was a grave digger by profession. He transmitted traditions regarding the pathology and growth of the human embryo.

Rabbi Abbahu was a second-generation (279–320) Palestinian *Amora* from Caesarea. He was a disciple of Rabbi Jochanan, a man of great wealth and of a liberal education. He had a thorough knowledge of Greek and favored Greek culture. He was held in high esteem by the Roman authorities and had great political influence. He seems to have had frequent controversies with the teachers of Christianity in Caesarea.

Rabbi Aha was a Palestinian *Amora* who lived in the fourth century. He is extensively quoted in the Jerusalem Talmud, but seldom in the Babylonian. His younger colleagues called him "the Light of Israel." He was merciful and gentle by nature. It is reported that on the day of his death, stars were visible at noontime.

Rabbi Akiba ben Joseph was one of the most prominent of the *Tannaim*. A third-generation *Tanna* (120–130), he grew up illiterate but became one of the most influential rabbis. He helped arrange the Mishnah into its present form. He also introduced a method of interpreting Scriptures that enabled him to find a biblical basis for almost every provision of the oral law. He died a martyr at the hands of the Romans for publicly teaching the Jewish tradition.

Rabbi Alexandri was a third-century Palestinian *Amora*. He was a leading aggadist of his day. It is related that he used to go about the streets of Lydda urging people to perform good deeds.

Rav Ammi bar Nathan was a Palestinian *Amora* who taught at the end of the third century. He and his colleague Rav Asi were the most outstanding Palestinian *Amoraim* of the period. Many stories are told of his piety, his scrupulousness in honoring Shabbat, and the miracles that happened to him (*Berachot* 62a).

Rav Ashi was a sixth-generation (375–427) Babylonian *Amora* who, at the age of 20, became president of the academy of Sura, which had been deserted for about 50 years. Under his presidency, which lasted 52 years, the academy regained its renown. He had great authority and was given the title *Rabbana* ("our teacher"). He helped to compile the Talmud.

Bar Hadaya was a dream interpreter who commuted between Palestine and Babylon and was active in the third and fourth generations of *Amoraim*.

Bar Kappara was a Palestinian scholar during the transition period between the *Tannaim* and the *Amoraim*, around the beginning of the third century C.E. He had an academy in Caesarea. He held original views, greatly valued the study of the natural sciences, and used the Greek language. He disliked metaphysical speculation and opposed Gnosticism and asceticism. He was a talented poet and authored many fables, epigrams, and prayers.

Beit Hillel and Beit Shammai, "the house of Hillel" and "the house of Shammai," existed from the end of the first century B.C.E. until the beginning of the second century C.E. In general, Beit Hillel was more lenient than its rival, Beit Shammai, but this is an oversimplification. One may safely say that Beit Shammai tended to interpret the Torah in a more literal, narrow way, whereas Beit Hillel tended to adopt a broader perspective on it. The opinions of Beit Hillel are almost always adopted over those of Beit Shammai.

Rav Chisda, a second-generation (257–320) Babylonian *Amora*, was a disciple of Rav. He became head of the academy in Sura when he was 80 years old and remained in that office for 10 years.

Rabbi Chiya the Elder (not the later *Amora* of the same name) was a Babylonian who became a sixth-generation *Tanna*. He came to Palestine when he had already reached an advanced age. Rabbi Chiya became the most distinguished disciple of Judah HaNasi, as well as his friend.

Chutspit the Turgeman was a third-generation *Tanna* and the announcer of Rabban Gamaliel in Yavneh. He was one of the ten martyrs who were killed during the Hadrianic persecutions.

Rav Dimi b. Abba may refer to Rav Dimi (b. Chinena) from Nehardea, who succeeded Rab Zebid in presiding over the school in Pumbedita for three years (385–388).

Rabbi Eleazar (ben Pedat), a third-century *Amora* who died in 279. Born in Babylonia, he was a member of a priestly family. There he studied under Samuel and Rav. After the latter's death, he immigrated to the Land of Israel. He was extremely poor. As well as being a great expounder of the oral law, he was a prolific and profound aggadist.

Rabbi Eleazar ben Azaria, a second-generation (80–120) *Tanna*, was a rabbi of great learning and nobility. After Rabban Gamaliel II was deposed from the presidency at Yavneh, Eleazar ben Azaria was chosen to take his place.

Eleazar ben Shammua, a *Tanna* from approximately 150. He was one of the last pupils of Rabbi Akiba and was one of the rabbis ordained by Judah ben Baba. Later midrashim include this Eleazar among the Ten Martyrs of the Hadrianic persecutions.

Rabbi Eliezer (ben Hyrkanos) was a second-generation (80–120) *Tanna*. He was a faithful conservator of decisions handed down from earlier generations and opposed even the slightest modification in them. He was an adherent of Beit Shammai, and thus frequently differed with his colleagues. Being persistent in his opinion, and conforming to it even in practice, he was excommunicated by his own brother-in-law, Gamaliel the II.

Elisha ben Abuya was a *Tanna* of the first half of the second century. He was born before the year 70. in Jerusalem, where his father was a prominent citizen. He rejected Judaism, although it is not clear exactly what religion he then adopted. He is also known as *Acher* or *Achor*, "the other."

Ezra was a priest and scribe who played a major role in rebuilding the Temple after the return from Babylonian exile. There is some debate over when he lived; the range extends from 465 to 359 B.C.E. He provided his community with a religious basis so that it could rebuild itself in Jerusalem. He adapted various laws in the Torah to the exigencies of the time.

Rabban Gamaliel was a second-generation *Tanna*. After the Second Temple was destroyed in 70, Jerusalem came under Roman occupation and could no longer function as the spiritual center for Judaism. Rabbi Johanan ben Zakkai therefore formed an academy in Yavneh to preserve the traditions of the Jewish people. After Johanan ben Zakkai died, Rabban Gamaliel became the president of the Academy. He wanted to secure Yavneh's status as the spiritual center of Judaism.

Hamnuna Saba ("the elder") was a Babylonian *Amora* of the mid-third century. He transmitted the sayings of his teacher, Rav, and succeeded Rav as the head of the academy of Sura. Many of his statements in the Talmud emphasize the duty to study Torah and the gravity of neglecting this *mitzvah*.

Rav Hamnuna Zuti ("the younger") was a Babylonian *Amora* of the fourth century and a pupil and colleague of Rav Hisda. He also studied under Rabbi Judah. He composed the confession of sin for the day of Atonement (see Chapter 2).

Rabbi Hanina ben Papa was a Palestinian *Amora* who lived at the end of the third and beginning of the fourth centuries. He immigrated to the Land of Israel in his youth and studied under Jochanan and others. He was renowned in the field of *aggadah* and was considered to be an excellent preacher. He was considered a paragon of holiness, and it is said that even the night spirits feared him. He is frequently mentioned together with Oshaya. They may have been brothers; both were sandal makers.

R. Hillel b. Samuel b. Nachmani was the son of Samuel ben Nachman, who lived in the late third and early fourth centuries. Samuel was a Palestinian *Amora* who studied under Rabbi Joshua ben Levi and Jonathan ben Eleazar. He was survived by two sons, Nachman and Hillel.

Rabbi Hiyya bar Abba was a third-generation Palestinian *Amora* (279–320). He immigrated from Babylonia with his brother Simon bar Abba and became a disciple of Rabbi Jochanan. He was a distinguished teacher, but very poor. He was inclined to rigorous views in questions of the law.

Hiyya bar Avin had a notable career. A Babylonian *Amora*, he lived in the beginning of the fourth century. He was held in such high respect that Rava referred to him as "the lion of the company." His discussions with his contemporary scholars are frequently cited in the Talmud.

Rav Huna (b. 212, d. 297) was a second-generation Babylonian *Amora*. He was president of the Academy at Sura for 40 years and had 800 disciples. He was highly revered for his great learning and his noble character. He enjoyed an undisputed authority, to which even some Palestinian teachers submitted.

Rabbi Isaac was a *Tanna* from Babylonia in the middle of the second century. He moved to the Land of Israel, where he debated the disciples of Rabbi Ishmael. He also engaged in mystical studies. He is not mentioned in the Mishnah but is often cited in *beraitot*.

Rabbi Jacob was probably a Babylonian-born *Amora* who lived around the end of the third and beginning of the fourth centuries.

Rabbi Jacob ben Idi, student of Rabbi Jochanan, received the teachings of the great sages of the first generation of Palestinian *Amoraim*.

Rabbi Jeremiah, a native of Babylonia, was a third-fourth generation (320–359) Palestinian *Amora* and a disciple of Rabbi Zeira. In his younger days, he indulged in posing puzzling questions of little import, probably intending to ridicule the dialectical methods used in the academies. For this reason, he was expelled from the academy. He then moved to the Land of Israel and was better appreciated there, being acknowledged as a great authority.

Rabbi Jochanan bar Napacha is usually called simply Rabbi Jochanan. He was born in about 199 and died in 279. He was a first-generation Palestinian *Amora*. He founded his own academy, which then became the principal seat of learning in the Land of Israel. He was regarded as the chief *Amora* of the Land of Israel due to his great mental powers.

Rabbi Jochanan HaSandlar was one of R. Akiba's last pupils. A *Tanna* of the first half of the second century, he is most frequently mentioned in the Mishnah and *beraitot* discussing *halachot* with Akiba's pupils or transmitting them in Akiba's name.

R. Jose b. Abin was a fourth-century Palestinian *Amora*. He played a large role in the final editing of the Jerusalem Talmud, which was completed in the following generations. He frequently transmitted the words of his predecessors. He is mentioned in the Babylonian Talmud, though at times his name is interchanged with that of his contemporary, **Jose ben Zevida**. There is confusion as to exactly when he lived.

Rabbi Jose (ben Chalafta), a fourth-generation (139–165) *Tanna* was a disciple of Rabbi Akiba. He was a great and fair-minded scholar, always trying to take every aspect of a problem into account. So great was his scholarship that whenever there is a conflict between him and his contemporaries, Rabbis Meir, Judah, and Simon, his opinion is always adopted. In addition to his intellectual gifts, he was also humble and righteous. It is said that Elijah was revealed to him every day.

Rav Joseph ben Hiyya (d. 333), a Babylonian *Amora*, headed the Pumbedita academy for two and a half years. Hundreds of his sayings are found throughout the Talmud. He was called *Sinai*, meaning a scholar with wide knowledge. He also delved into mysticism. He was renowned for his high ethical standards and especially for his humility. A wealthy man, he supported 400 of his pupils.

Rabbi Joshua (ben Chanania) belonged to the second generation of *Tannaim* (80–120). Joshua often had discussions with Rabbi Eliezer, his rational and conciliatory style contrasting with Rabbi Eliezer's unyielding conservatism. It was on Rabbi Joshua's account that Nasi Gamaliel II was removed from office.

Rabbi Joshua ben Korcha was a fourth-generation *Tanna*. Although an authority of that generation, only a few of his opinions are recorded in the Mishnah.

Rabbi Joshua ben Levi was a second-generation (219–279) Palestinian *Amora* (b. around 180, d. 260). He is regarded as a great authority in the law, and his decisions often prevail over those of Rabbi Jochanan and Reish Lakish, his two great contemporaries. He was also a prolific aggadist. He presided over an academy in Lydda. It is said that, on one occasion, his prayer for rain was efficacious, and this later gave rise to many mystic legends about him.

Rabbi Josiah was a Palestinian *Amora* who lived in the third century. He was a pupil of Rabbi Jochanan and Rabbi Kahana, and was held in high esteem by his contemporaries. When Isaac b. Redifa came to ask a halachic question of Jeremiah, the latter replied, "the lions are available and you inquire of the foxes! Go and ask Josiah" (Talmud Yerushalmi, *Shevuot* 9:5, 39a). A number of *Amoraim* with the name Josiah are mentioned in the Talmud.

Rav Judah (bar Yecheskel), a second-generation (257–320) Babylonian *Amora,* was a disciple of both Rav's and Shmuel's. He founded the academy in Pumbedita and also headed the academy at Sura for the two years before his death in 299.

Rabbi Judah ben Baba, a third-generation (120–139) *Tanna* was also called the *Chasid* (the righteous one) on account of his piety. He was a distinguished teacher and was martyred by the Romans for ordaining seven disciples of Rabbi Akiba as rabbis.

Rabbi Juda (ben Bathyra) already had a school in Nisibis, Assyria, when the Temple still stood. He was a second-generation (80–120) *Tanna.*

Rabbi Judah HaNasi, simply called Rabbi, or our Rabbi, a fifth-generation (165–200) *Tanna*, was a son of the patriarch Rabbi Simon ben Gamaliel II. He was well versed not only in the traditional law, but also in secular subjects, such as the Greek language. He became the chief authority of his generation. Although personally wealthy, he lived simply and sustained many students by his charity. He is said to have been in a friendly relation with one of the Roman emperors. He completed the compilation of the Mishnah begun by Rabbi Akiba.

R. Levi bar Hama was a Palestinian *Amora* of the third quarter of the third century. Like Reish Lakish, he had strong ties to R. Jochanan. He lectured in Jochanan's academy for 22 years and was known for his ability to interpret a text in many different ways. He is known more for his *aggadot* than for his determination of the law.

Mar bar Ravina was a fourth-century Babylonian *Amora*, famous for his saintly character. Although wealthy, he lived austerely and with great piety. At his son's nuptials he deliberately broke a precious cup to bring the overly boisterous crowd back to their senses. The destruction of the Temple influenced him deeply.

Rabbi Meir was a fourth-generation (139–165) *Tanna*. His ordination was confirmed by Rabbi Judah ben Baba, after he had been ordained by Rabbi Akiba quite early in his (Meir's) career. He was the most prominent of Rabbi Akiba's disciples and continued Rabbi Akiba's work in arranging the material of the oral law according to subjects. In this way he helped prepare the great Mishnah compilation of Judah HaNasi. Rabbi Meir's legal opinions are mentioned in almost every book of the Mishnah.

Rav Nachman bar Isaac, a third-generation (320–375) Babylonian *Amora*, was president of the academy in Pumbedita for four years (352–356) and left no remarkable traces of his activity.

Rabbi Nathan (The Babylonian), a fifth-generation (165–200) *Tanna*, came from an aristocratic family in Babylon. He emigrated to Judea and, on account of his great learning, was appointed vice-president of the Sanhedrin in Usha. He was also well versed in mathematics, astronomy, and other sciences.

Rabbi Nehemiah was a fourth-generation (139–165) *Tanna* and one of the last disciples of Rabbi Akiba. He was an authority on the laws of the sacrifices and levitical purification. His controversies are mostly with Rabbi Judah bar Ilai. He is said to have compiled a collection of Mishnayot which is embodied in the *Tosefta*.

Rabbi Oshaiah may be **Oshaiah Rabbah**, a Palestinian *Amora* of the first half of the second century who was a member of Rabbi Judah HaNasi's council in Sepphoris. He was famed for his collection of *beraitot* and his ability to explain them. This name may also refer to **Rav Hoshaiah**, a Babylonian *Amora* of the end of the third and the beginning of the fourth centuries. He was a cobbler by trade and was well known for his piety and righteousness.

Rav Papa (bar Chanan), a fifth-generation (320–375) Babylonian *Amora*, was a disciple of Abaye and Rava. He adopted their dialectical method but did not possess their ingenuity and independence in applying it.

Pappus b. Judah was a *Tanna* from the end of the first and beginning of the second centuries. He was distinguished for his pious character and conducted himself with special stringency. He would lock his wife indoors when he went out so that she would not talk to other people.

Rabba bar bar Chana was a Babylonian *Amora* of the second generation (257–320). He attended R. Jochanan's academy in Tiberias, in the Land of Israel and then returned to Babylonia. He is noted for the many allegorical narratives ascribed to him in the Talmud (such as the one in Chapter 8).

Rabba (bar Nachmani) was a Babylonian *Amora* who lived from 270 until 330. He was a disciple of Rav Chisda, among others, and had great analytical and intellectual powers. He became the head of the academy of Pumbedita and attracted large crowds at his lectures there. He lived a life of poverty and persecuted by the Babylonian authorities, he suffered a tragic death.

Rav is also known as Abba Areca and Abba bar Ino. He was born in around 175 and died in 247, and was a first-generation Babylonian *Amora*. He was regarded as a semi-*Tanna* and was thus able to dispute some opinions accepted in the Mishnah, a privilege not accorded to any other *Amora*.

Rava, a fourth-generation Babylonian *Amora*, was born in 299 and died in 352. He was a colleague of Abaye, and developed dialectical powers that soon surpassed those of any of his contemporaries. His rulings overrule Abaye's in all but six cases in the Talmud. His academy in Machuza supplanted all others in Babylonia.

Ravin was a Babylonian *Amora* who lived around 300. He immigrated to the Land of Israel to study and brought the teachings of that land back to Babylonia.

Reish Lakish. See Rabbi Simon ben Lakish

Mar Samuel (or Shmuel) was born around 180 in Nehardea and died there in 257. A first-generation Babylonian *Amora* (219–257), like his colleague Rav, he went to the Land of Israel and there became a disciple of Judah HaNasi, although Judah did not ordain him. Samuel was interested in medicine and astronomy. Although he and Rav often differed on questions of law, their relationship was friendly. After Rav's death in 247, Samuel became the highest religious authority in Babylonia.

Rav Shesheth, a Babylonian *Amora* of the second generation, opposed hair-splitting methods of study and often opposed Rav Chisda. He was blind, and thus had to depend on his powerful memory.

Rabbi Shimon ben Pazzi was a Palestinian *Amora* who lived in the second half of the third century. He was basically an aggadist.

Rabbi Simeon bar Yochai was a fourth-generation (139–165) *Tanna* from the Galilee. He was one of Rabbi Akiba's most distinguished disciples. Persecuted by the Romans, he hid himself in a cave for several years with his son, eating only carob to sustain himself. He opened an academy in Tekoa in the Galilee once the Roman government stopped persecuting him. He followed the school of R. Ishmael rather than Akiba's more fanciful method. He is regarded as the author of *Sifrei*, the midrash on Deuteronomy.

Simeon ben Azzai was a *Tanna* of the early second century who lived in Tiberias. In order to devote himself to the study of Torah, he never married. He was one of the four who "entered the garden" of mystical speculation and died as a result of this experience. He was an outstanding scholar and was renowned for his saintliness.

Rabbi Simon ben Lakish (known as **Reish Lakish**) lived in Palestine and was a second generation *Amora* (219–279). Before becoming a scholar, he was a gladiator for the Romans. He had extraordinary intellectual and analytical gifts. He was not only good friends with Rav Jochanan but his brother-in-law as well.

Simeon ben Zoma was a second-century *Tanna*. He apparently was not ordained a rabbi but was nonetheless considered an outstanding scholar. He was interested in mystical speculation and was said to have either died or become demented after one particularly intense mystical encounter, recounted in *Hagigah* 14b.

Symmachus, a fifth-generation (165–200) *Tanna*, was a prominent disciple of Rabbi Meir's and was distinguished for his great dialectical powers. After Meir's death, however, he was excluded from Rabbi Judah HaNasi's school, charged with indulging in disputes designed to show off his intellect rather than seeking the truth.

R. Tanhum (ben Hiyya) was a Palestinian *Amora* of the end of the third and beginning of the fourth centuries. Tanhum was wealthy and charitable. It is told that all human statues were dislodged when he died.

Rabbi Tarphon belonged to the third generation of *Tannaim* (120–139) and was inclined to follow the views of Beit Shammai. He was a man of great learning who held most of his discussions with Rabbi Akiba.

Ulla was a Palestinian *Amora* of the second half of the third century. He studied under Rabbi Jochanan bar Napacha, Reish Lakish, and Rabbi Eleazar ben Pedat. He was extremely strict in his interpretation of religious laws and denigrated decisions he disliked. He was greatly respected in the Land of Israel and in Babylonia, which he visited frequently. He felt the tragedy of the destruction of the Temple deeply. He died in Babylon, survived by his only son, Rabba.

Rabbi Zadok was a second-generation (80–120) *Tanna* who taught in Yavneh. It is told that in anticipation of the destruction of the Temple, he fasted for 40 years.

Rabbi Zera was a second-generation (279–320) Palestinian *Amora*. He was a Babylonian but did not like the hair-splitting techniques of study used in the academies there, so he immigrated to the Land of Israel where he was ordained.

Rab Zebid (b. Oshaya) presided over the academy in Pumbedita, Babylonia for eight years (377–385). He was a fourth-generation (375–427) Babylonian *Amora*.

Mar Zutra was an *Amora* of the fourth generation (375–427) in Pumbedita, Babylonia.

Appendix II: Halachah

The following is a translation of Steinsaltz's (1983) summary of the *halachah* for this tractate. (Used with permission.)

Chapter 1

2a: Evening is considered to have commenced when the sun has gone down and three stars are visible (*Shulchan Aruch, Orach Chayim* 235:1).

The actual obligation to say the *Shema* extends until dawn, but you should do it before midnight (*Shulchan Aruch, Orach Chayim* 235:3).

3a: We ought not enter into a ruin to pray, or for any other reason, because of three things: (1) because it may appear that we enter the area for an illicit sexual liaison, (2) because the walls may fall in on us, and/or (3) because evil spirits may lurk there (Rambam, *Mishneh Torah, Sefer Nezikin, Hilchot Rotseiach V'Shmirat HaNefesh*, ch. 2, no. 6).

6b: One may even run to hear words of Torah on Shabbat. (*Shulchan Aruch, Orach Chayim* 301:1).

11b: Every morning one says each of these three blessings over the Torah. We are obligated to say a blessing for Torah when we are engaged in any activity that has any aspect of Torah learning to it (*Shulchan Aruch, Orach Chayim* 60:2 and 47:8).

Chapter 2

13a: If one is reading the *Shema* in the Torah at the time when it is to be read, and does so with intention, then one has

173

fulfilled one's obligation to recite the *Shema* (*Shulchan Aruch, Orach Chayim* 60:5).

Mitzvot require *kavanah*, intention, for one to fulfill one's obligation (*Shulchan Aruch, Orach Chayim* 60:4).

One may give greetings to an honored person and receive greetings from anyone in between the paragraphs of the *Shema*. One may pause in the middle of a paragraph out of fear—either fear in terms of honoring someone, such as a parent or teacher, or fear in the sense of concern that the individual might harm one if not greeted. The breaks are between each blessing and between the portions of the *Shema*. However, no break is made between the last word of the *Shema* and the first word of the next prayer, *Emet v'Yatsiv* or *Emet v'Emunah* (*Shulchan Aruch, Orach Chayim* 66:1,8).

15a: One must recite the *Shema* so that one hears it with one's own ears. However, if one did not hear it, one has nevertheless fulfilled one's obligation (*Shulchan Aruch, Orach Chayim* 62:3).

Similarly, if one did not say the words exactly, one has still fulfilled one's obligation (*Shulchan Aruch, Orach Chayim* 62:1).

However, one must read the paragraphs in the correct order (*Shulchan Aruch, Orach Chayim* 64:1). If one makes a mistake in the recitation of the *Shema*, one has not fulfilled one's obligation and must repeat the recitation (*Shulchan Aruch, Orach Chayim* 62:5).

The *Shema* may be recited in the language one understands (Rambam, *Mishneh Torah, Sefer Ahavah*, Chapter 2, no. 10).

16a: One may recite the *Shema* while standing in the top of a tree or in a similar situation (*Shulchan Aruch, Orach Chayim* 63:8).

Grooms are no longer exempt from saying the *Shema* on their wedding night or for three days afterward if they still have not consummated the marriage (*Shulchan Aruch, Orach Chayim* 70:3).

One may say the *Tefillah* in olive and fig trees, although not in other species of trees. No matter what kind of tree, the master of the house descends from the tree to pray (*Shulchan Aruch, Orach Chayim* 90:3).

17a: Women are rewarded (by God) for facilitating the Torah study of their husbands and children (*Smichat Chachamim* and *Rif*, Rabbi Isaiah Pinto).

"Generally, women and slaves are exempt from positive commandments caused by time, although there are some time-related positive commandments which women are required to perform, for example, remembering the Sabbath day to keep it holy, eating *matzah* on Passover night, 'public assembly,' and prayer" (Steinsaltz 1989, p. 222). Some authorities obligate women to say the first line of the *Shema* (Deuteronomy 6:4; *Shulchan Aruch, Orach Chayim* 70:1).

Chapter 3

17b: Mourners are exempt from the obligation to recite the *Shema* and *Tefillah* and from all the other *mitzvot* until their dead are buried. Mourners are the children, parents, siblings, and spouse of the deceased (*Shulchan Aruch, Yoreh De'ah* 341).

19b: Those who stand in a line to see and comfort the mourners are exempt from the obligation to recite the *Shema*. Others who do not see the mourners are still obligated to recite the *Shema* (*Shulchan Aruch, Orach Chayim* 72:8).

20a: Children who have begun their education should say the *Shema* (*Shulchan Aruch, Orach Chayim* 70:2).

20b: Women, slaves, and minors are exempt from the obligation to don *tefillin* (*Shulchan Aruch, Orach Chayim* 38:3).

Everyone, including women and slaves, is obligated to put a *mezuzah* on his or her door, and minors are to be educated on the importance of this *mitzvah* (*Shulchan Aruch, Yoreh De'ah* 291:1).

Similarly, everyone is obligated to say the *Tefillah* and educate minors as to its importance (*Shulchan Aruch, Yoreh De'ah* 186:1, 2).

Similarly, everyone is obligated to say *Birkat HaMazon* (*Shulchan Aruch, Yoreh De'ah* 271:2).

One who is not obligated to do a certain *mitzvah* may not fulfill it on behalf of someone else. (Rambam, *Mishneh Torah, Sefer Ahavah, Hilchot Berachot*, Chapter 1, no. 11).

22a: Today, even a person who is ritually impure may study Torah and touch holy objects (*Shulchan Aruch, Yoreh De'ah* 282:9).

23a: Today, we are prohibited from taking *tefillin* into a bathroom (*Shulchan Aruch, Yoreh De'ah* 43:1).

Chapter 4

26a: One should recite the morning *Tefillah* before a third of the day has passed (up until the fourth hour); however, *ex post facto*, it is acceptable until noon (*Shulchan Aruch, Orach Chayim* 89:1).

One may say the afternoon prayer until evening (*Shulchan Aruch, Orach Chayim* 108:1,2).

One may recite the additional service (*musaf*) until the seventh hour; however, *ex post facto*, one may recite it at any time during the day (*Shulchan Aruch, Orach Chayim* 286:8).

The evening prayer may be said from sunset until dawn. (*Rambam, Mishneh Torah, Sefer Ahavah*, Chapter 3, no. 6).

26b: The *Tefillot* are in place of the sacrifices. There are many similarities between the two activities: they are both to be done in a constant place; one's thoughts may invalidate one's plea, and so on. (*Shulchan Aruch, Orach Chayim* 95:4).

27b: The evening *Tefillah* is not mandatory. (Rambam, Mishneh Torah, Sefer Ahavah, Hilchot Tefillah, Chapter 1, no. 6).

One who publicly shames another loses one's place in the World to Come unless one performs the appropriate *teshuvah*. (See *Baba Metsiah*, p. 58b and Rambam, *Mishneh Torah, Sefer Madah, Hilchot Teshuvah*, Chapter 3, no. 14).

One must take great care not to oppress a proselyte to Judaism; for example, one must not remind proselytes that they once were not Jewish. (See *Baba Metsia* 58b and 59b; *Shulchan Aruch, Choshen Mishpat* 228:2).

When something becomes separated or lost, it is considered to belong to the majority group that surrounds it. The classic example is when you find a piece of meat on the street and there are nine kosher butcher shops and one nonkosher butcher shop on that street, you may assume that the piece of meat is kosher. (*Ketubot* 15a; *Shulchan Aruch, Yoreh De'ah* 110:3).

28a: Today the residents of the territories that belonged to Amon and Moab are allowed to convert to Judaism (*Shulchan Aruch, Even Haezer* 4:10).

28b: One who can recite the *Tefillah* fluently should say it in its entirety. If one cannot, or it is a time of danger, one may recite the shortened version (*Havineinu*) (*Shulchan Aruch, Orach Chayim* 110:1).

One does not recite *Havineinu* during the winter, when we pray for rain, or on Saturday night at the end of Shabbat (*Shulchan Aruch, Orach Chayim* 110:1).

29b: At a time of danger, one says the version of the short *Tefillah* offered by "others" in this *sugya*. One need not say the first three blessings or last three blessings of the *Amidah* with this *Tefillah*. However, once one has reached safety, one then recites the full *Tefillah* (*Shulchan Aruch, Orach Chayim* 100:2).

Chapter 5

30b: It is fitting to say the *Tefillah* out of seriousness and fear, not out of lightheadedness (*Shulchan Aruch, Orach Chayim* 93:2).

31a: A *shaliach tsibbur*, one who leads the congregation in prayer, does not stretch out his prayer to the point that it becomes a burden on the community (*Shulchan Aruch, Orach Chayim* 23:11).

One should pronounce the words of the *Tefillah* quietly and not just mumble them (*Shulchan Aruch, Orach Chayim* 110:2). One should not say the *Tefillah* while drunk. One should wait until one becomes sober (*Shulchan Aruch, Orach Chayim* 79:1).

32b: One does not break off in the middle of the *Tefillah* to greet any Jew, even a Jewish king. However, one may break off to greet a non-Jew. However, it is better to shorten the prayer rather than interrupt it (*Shulchan Aruch, Orach Chayim* 104:1).

33b: One who says "We give thanks, we give thanks" or mentions God's mercy on a bird's nest is taken away from leading the prayers (Rambam, *Sefer Ahavah, Hilchot Tefillah*, Chapter 9, no. 9).

We do not add to the praises of God written in the prayer book. We are permitted to do so in our private supplications (*Shulchan Aruch, Orach Chayim* 113:9).

34a: One makes one's requests during the middle prayers of the *Tefillah*. (*Shulchan Aruch, Orach Chayim* 112:1).

We bow at the beginning and end of the first *berachah* of the *Amidah (Avot)* and at the beginning and end of the prayer of thanks (*Hoda'ah*) (*Shulchan Aruch, Orach Chayim* 113:1).

34b: Those who sin and repent have greater merit than the wholly righteous (Rambam, *Mishneh Torah, Hilchot Teshuvah,* Chapter 7, no. 4).

Chapter 6

35a: We should try to remember the source of what we eat in our *berachah*. However, if we cannot remember and so say the catch-all *berachah*, " . . . by whose word all things exist," it is satisfactory. The difference between the fruit of the tree and the fruit of the ground is obvious: the fruit of the tree may be included in the fruit of the ground, but not vice versa. Wine and bread have blessings specifically designated for them.

We make a blessing before eating anything (*Shulchan Aruch, Orach Chayim* 210:1).

40b: One should not change the formula of the *berachot* laid down by the sages, but ex post facto, if one mentioned the main features of a blessing (God's name and God's kingship), one has fulfilled one's obligation (Rambam, *Mishneh Torah, Sefer Ahavah, Hilchot Berachot,* Chapter 1, no. 5). One may make a blessing in any language as long as it is an accurate translation of Hebrew (Rambam, *Mishneh Torah, Sefer Ahavah,* Chapter 1, no. 6).

41a: When faced with several varieties of food, one may choose which law to follow when deciding which food to bless first. The majority of authorities seem to suggest that one should bless that which one likes best first, while others suggest that one blesses a food that is one of the seven varieties (wheat, barley, grapes, figs, pomegranates, olives, and honey) mentioned in the Torah first (*Shulchan Aruch, Orach Chayim* 211:1).

43b: A sage should not behave in any way that brings shame upon himself (that is, dressing in perfumed clothes) or go out in the evening unless he does so regularly and for a clearly legitimate purpose (Rambam, *Mishneh Torah, Sefer Ha-Madah, Hilchot Deiot*, Chapter 5, no. 9).

Chapter 7

45a: Three persons who have eaten together are obligated to say *zimmun* before *Birkat HaMazon*.

One may say *zimmun* over *demai* and over the first tithe from which *terumah* has been removed as well as over the second tithe (Rambam, *Mishneh Torah, Sefer Ahavah, Hilchot Berachot*, Chapter 5, no. 2).

One is included in the invitation only if one has eaten an olive's worth of food (0.9 fluid ounce, according to Carmell [1980]).

We do not include non-Jews, women, slaves, or minors in the *zimmun* (*Shulchan Aruch, Orach Chayim* 199:4,6).

45b: Women and slaves may invite each other to say grace when they are in groups by themselves (*Shulchan Aruch, Orach Chayim* 199:6).

46a: Guests lead the *Birkat HaMazon* (*Shulchan Aruch, Orach Chayim* 167:14).

34a: If one is asked to act as *shaliach tsibbur*, one should at first demur and then agree to do so (*Shulchan Aruch, Orach Chayim* 53:16). (This law refers to a person who does not serve as a permanent *shaliach tsibbur.*)

47a: The greatest person present says *Birkat HaMazon*, even when that person came in at the end of the meal (*Shulchan Aruch, Yoreh De'ah* 201:1).

Pesachim 25a,b: We are required to martyr ourselves rather than do three things: practice idolatry, kill another person, or commit sexual sins such as incest or adultery (Rambam, *Mishneh Torah, Sefer HaMadah, Hilchot Yesodei HaTorah*, Chapter 5, no. 7).

47b: Today we include even *amei ha-arets* in *zimmun*, unless they have removed themselves from the Jewish people (*Shulchan Aruch, Orach Chayim* 199:3).

48a: A minor who knows to whom a blessing is addressed may be included for *zimmun* if he is 7 or some say 9 years old. However, others insist that he reach his majority before he is included (*Shulchan Aruch, Orach Chayim* 199:10).

49b: When three or more persons recite *zimmun* they say, "Let us bless" (or "Bless" when four are present). When ten or more are present, the *zimmun* begins, "Let us bless our God." There is no difference in this formula whether there are ten or more than ten persons present who are eligible for *zimmun* (*Shulchan Aruch, Orach Chayim* 192:1).

Chapter 8

Baba Metsia 59b: It is said in the Torah "It is not in the heavens" to imply that no prophet can come now and revise the laws of the Torah. Even if this prophet makes signs and miracles and says that God sends him, we do not change the *mitzvot* on his account (Rambam, *Mishneh Torah, Sefer HaMadah, Hilchot Yesodei HaTorah*, Chapter 9, no. 1.

51b: One says the blessing over the wine and then the blessing over the day when saying Kiddush.

53b: The authorities disagree as to whether one must return to the place where one has eaten. There are those who say that one who forgot by mistake need not return, but that one who "forgot" on purpose must return. However, *ex post facto*, if one says *Birkat HaMazon*, one has fulfilled one's obligation. And there are those who say that even one who forgot by mistake must return to the place where one ate to say grace, but that one who did not return has fulfilled one's obligation. In general, one should always return to the place where one ate in order to say grace. However, one need only say the grace to fulfill one's obligation (*Shulchan Aruch, Orach Chayim* 184:1).

Chapter 9

54a: One who sees a place where miracles were wrought for Israel says the blessing, "Blessed are You . . . who performed miracles for our fathers in this place" (*Shulchan Aruch, Orach Chayim* 218:1).

The blessings for shooting stars, earthquakes, mountains, over any ocean, not just the Mediterranean, rain, and good and bad tidings are as noted in the Mishnah.

58b: One who sees a friend after a lapse of 30 days recites the prayer "Blessed are You . . . who has kept us alive, sustained us, and brought us to this time" (the *Shehechiyanu*) (*Shulchan Aruch, Orach Chayim* 228:1).

One who sees a person of unusual appearance, who looked that way from birth, says the blessing " . . . who creates various creatures." One who sees a person of unusual appearance who looks this way because something in his or her life has changed says the blessing " . . . the True Judge."

60a: We do not pray to change things once they have already occurred, even when the outcome is not known to us (e.g., praying for a child of a certain gender once a pregnancy has begun) (*Shulchan Aruch, Orach Chayim* 230:1).

60b: It is fitting for one to accept the bad things that come to one in faith, just as one accepts the good things that come to one (*Shulchan Aruch, Orach Chayim* 222:3).

Glossary

Additional Prayers: See *Musaf.*

A Fortiori: See *Kal va'Homer.*

Aggadah/Aggadot: Stories in the Talmud text as opposed to material pertaining directly to Jewish law. Differs from *midrash* in that these stories are not necessarily related to a Torah text. (Example of an *aggadah*: the story about the two spirits in the cemetery in Chapter 3.)

Aggadic: Of, or concerning, *aggadah.*

Aggadist: A teller of stories. One who interprets the Torah text rather than concentrating on *halachah*, "Jewish law."

Am Ha-arets/Amei ha-arets: Literally, "a people of the land." An idiom designating a Jewishly unlearned person and/or a person who behaves boorishly. Steinsaltz (1989) defines an *am ha-arets* in Mishnaic times as "an ignorant person who is not scrupulous in his observance of the commandments . . . The opposite of an *um ha-arets* is a *chaver* . . . Towards the end of the Mishnaic period most of the restrictions governing the *am ha-arets* were rescinded, partly out of fear of causing division within the Jewish people and partly because there was a significant improvement in the religious observance of the masses" (p. 241).

Amidah/Amidot/Tefillah/Tefillot/Shemonah Esrei: Literally, "standing," "the prayer," and "eighteen." The preeminent prayer in Judaism. It contains nineteen benedictions and is said standing three times each day.

Amora/Amoraim: The sages who expounded the Mishnah and thereby composed the Gemara. The Gemara and Mishnah together form the Talmud. The period of the *Amoraim* extends from the death of Judah HaNasi until the Babylonian Talmud was compiled—that is from the end of the third to the end of the fifth century. *Amoraim* lived in both the Land of Israel and Babylonia.

Arakhin: "Valuations." A tractate of the Babylonian Talmud.

Aramaic: One of the languages used in the Talmud. It is similar in some ways to Hebrew. It developed after Hebrew and was the language of the general population in the days of the rabbis.

Av Beit Din: Literally, "the father of the court." This was the title held by the vice-president of the Sanhedrin. The president was called the *nasi*.

B.C.E.: Before the Common Era; that is B.C.

Ba'al Keri/Ba'alei Keri: Literally, "master of an accident." A man who becomes ritually impure through an emission of semen, intentionally, unintentionally, or during sexual intercourse.

Baba Batra: Literally, "the last gate." A tractate of the Talmud in the Order of *Nezikin*, Damages. Its topic is civil law.

Baba Metsia: Literally, "the middle gate." A tractate of the Talmud in the Order of *Nezikin*, Damages. Its topic is civil law.

Baraita/Baraitot: Literally, "external." A source from the Tannaitic era that was not included in the Mishnah of Rabbi Judah HaNasi but is cited by the *Amoraim*.

Baruch: "Blessed."

Bat Kol: Literally, "A Voice from Heaven." There are four possible meanings for this concept: (1) Popular opinion; (2) Listening to children, especially asking them what verse they are reading and taking it as prophecy; (3) An echo: *bat kol* can be taken literally as "the daughter of a sound"; (4) *Bat Kol Min HaShamayim*: A voice from heaven. This is true revelation; however it cannot be used as a basis for adjudicating Jewish law.

Bavli: "Babylonian." The Talmud composed in Babylonia.

Bechorot: "The first-born ones." A tractate of the Talmud outlining the laws concerning first-born male animals and human beings.

Beit HaKneset: Literally, "the house of meeting." A synogogue.

Beit HaMidrash: Literally, "the house of expounding." An academy of rabbinic learning.

Beit Hillel: Literally, "the house of Hillel." The school that developed to expound the ideas of Hillel, one of the last of the *zugot*. The laws of this school are almost always adopted over those of Beit Shammai. These two houses existed during the first generation of *Tannaim* (10–80 C.E.).

Beit Shammai: Literally, "the house of Shammai." The school that developed to expound the ideas of Shammai, one of the last of the *zugot*.

Berachah/Berachot: A blessing. Must usually contain the formula "Blessed is the Lord our God, Ruler of the universe..."

Berachah L'vatalah: A vain prayer. Either the requisite *mitzvah* was not performed with it or it is said over something for which it is not proper to pray (e.g. praying that a fetus will be male after the pregnancy is more than 40 days old).

Birkat HaMazon: The blessing over food said after a meal. It is derived from Deuteronomy 8:10, "When you have eaten and are satisfied, you will bless the Lord Your God for the good land He has given you."

Birkot Hanehenim: Blessings for enjoyments such as pleasant fragrances, marvels of nature, and so on.

Birkot HaShachar: Blessings of the morning to be said as we become aware of our world after waking (thanking God for clothes to wear, our souls, and so on). These prayers are now said in synagogue as an introduction to the regular service.

C.E.: The Common Era (A.D.).

Chaver: An associate or colleague. The opposite of an *Am Haarets*. Someone who was dedicated to the strict observance of the *mitzvot*, particularly the payments of "Jewish taxes" and the laws of ritual purity.

Cherubim: Angels.

Chol: Secular; profane; not holy.

Chuppah: A wedding canopy. Also used to refer to marriage in general.

Coved Rosh: "Heavy headedness." Seriousness; proper deportment.

Cutean: A Samaritan. The Samaritans believed only in certain portions of the Written Torah, and not at all in the Oral one.

Demai: Literally, "suspicion." Food that was purchased from a person who may not have taken out the tithes as required by Jewish law.

Derech Erets: Literally, "the way of the land." Good manners. May also refer to making a living.

Din: Literally, "judgment." The strict letter of the law. Usually contrasted with *Lifnim Mishurat HaDin*.

DeOraita: "From the Torah." A law derived from the Torah.

DeRabbanan: "From our rabbis." A law of rabbinic origin.

Dinar/Dinarii: Also known as *zuzim*. Silver coins.

Drash: The act of making an exposition of a biblical text.

Drasha/Drashot: An exposition of a biblical text.

Ecclesiastes: One of the five scrolls. A book of wisdom literature.

First Tithe: *Ma'aser rishon* in Hebrew. When a crop is harvested, first *terumah* is set aside (one-fortieth to one-sixtieth of the total harvest). Then this first tithe (i.e., one-tenth of the remaining crop) is set aside for the Levites. The *second tithe* is an additional part of the crop set aside after *terumah* and the first tithe have been taken out. This produce was to be consumed in Jerusalem or traded for money, which was then spent on food in Jerusalem. This tithe was collected during the first, second, fourth, and fifth years of the Sabbatical cycle.

Gemara: The commentary on the Mishnah, composed by the *Amoraim*. It contains *baraitot, aggadot,* and *Amoraic* discussions. The Babylonian Gemara was formulated between 200 and 500 C.E.

Gehenna/Gehinnom: A place of punishment or unpleasantness in the afterlife.

Gezeira Shava: "An equivalent pronouncement." "An analogy of expressions based on identical or similar words occurring in two different passages of Scripture" (Mielziner 1968, p. 143).

Gnosticism: A dualistic religion that holds that there are two gods, a god of good and a god of evil.

Great Assembly: *Kenesset HaGedolah*. The legislative body of the *sofrim*, the scribes, which preceded the Sanhedrin of the Pharisees.

Haftarah: From the root dismiss or release. A reading from the Prophets that follows the Torah readings on Shabbats and Festivals.

Haggadah: The book used as a service for the first night(s) of Pesach.

Hagigah: A tractate of the Babylonian Talmud.

Hagiographa: The Writings. The third part of the Tanach containing the Psalms, Proverbs, Job, the Five Scrolls, Daniel, Ezra, Nehemiah, and Chronicles.

Halachah: "The way." Jewish law.

Halachah K'vatraei: "The law is like the last ones." The concept that in the development of Jewish law, the decisions of the latest generation of scholars are those that are accepted in practice.

Hallel/Hallel of Egypt: "Praise." Psalms 113–118 recited on Festivals, Channukah, and new moons. The Hallel of Egypt is the Hallel as it is recited on the eve of Passover (Psalm 136 is added at the end).

Havdalah: "Difference." The ceremony that concludes the Sabbath on Saturday evening. Prayers are said over wine, spices, and a braided candle.

Havineinu: "Grant us." The first word of the abridgement of the middle section of the *Amidah*. The first three blessings are said, then this paragraph, then the last three blessings.

Hitlahavut: To be excited or on fire. A burning desire for Torah knowledge.

Ishah Chashuvah: "An important woman." A special category comprising women who were apparently wealthy enough to be freed from many household responsibilities and had a slightly different status under Jewish law regarding some selected *mitzvot*.

Kabbalat Shabbat: "Welcoming the Sabbath." An opening service before the Friday evening worship proper. It was introduced in the sixteenth century by Kabbalists (mystics) in Safed, Palestine.

Kaddish: Holy in Aramaic. A prayer of praise to God recited at funerals, during mourning, after communal study, between major sections of a worship service, and at other times.

Kalut Rosh: Light headedness. Frivolousness; insufficient seriousness. The opposite of *coved rosh*, "heavy headedness," or seriousness.

Kal va'Homer: An *a fortiori* inference; a logical comparison between two cases, one lenient (*kal*) and the other strict (*homer*): "If A, then certainly B." For example, "If you have run with foot-soldiers and they have wearied you, how can you contend with horses?" (Jeremiah 12:5). (See Steinsaltz 1989, p. 153, for a good, lengthy discussion of this concept.)

Katan: A minor or person who has not reached maturity, generally accepted as up to the age of 12 for girls and 13 for boys.

Kavanah: Intention; concentration during prayer and/or doing a *mitzvah* for the right reason (that is, love of God).

Kevah: Permanence; "regularity." Usually refers to an obligation that is set, that must be fulfilled regularly, (e.g., the obligation to say the *Shema* twice a day). Often in tension with the concept *kavanah* (intention).

Kiddush HaShem: "The sanctification of the Name." Martyrdom.

Kiddush (Kedushat HaYom): "The holiness of the day." The prayer said to sanctify Shabbat and festivals. Said during the *Amidah* and over wine (for example, on Shabbat eve).

Kodesh: Holy. Opposite of *chol*.

Kriat Shema: "The reading of the *Shema*." The reading of the *Shema*, Hear; the central creed of Judaism. Consists of Deuteronomy 6:4–9, Deuteronomy 11:13–21, and Numbers 15:37–41. The first line must be said with intention.

Lifnim Mishurat Hadin: "Inside the line of justice." Going beyond the letter of the law; acting according to ethical standards that are higher than what is dictated by *halachah*.

Ma'ariv: Evening. The evening prayers at which the *Shema* and *Amidah* are recited.

Ma'asim Tovim: Good deeds.

Masechet/Masechtot: Tractate. A volume of Talmud or Mishnah.

Menachot: Meal offerings. A tractate of the Talmud dealing with various meal offerings and the laws of *tsitsit, mezuzah,* and *tefillin*. It is in the Order *Kodoshim*.

Mensch/Menschen: Yiddish meaning "a person"; someone who acts decently, fairly, and ethically.

Menschlichkeit: The end product of acting like a *mensch*. Fairness; decency.

Mezuzah: Doorpost. A parchment on which are written the words of Deuteronomy 6:4–9 and Deuteronomy 11:13–21. The parchment is then encased and affixed to the doorpost of a dwelling.

Minchah: Afternoon. The afternoon recitation of the *Amidah*.

Min/Minim: "Kind or species." A heretic, especially members of early Jewish Christian sects or Gnostics.

Minor: See *katan*.

Mishnah/Mishnayot: Teaching. Refers to the collection of Tannaitic learning compiled by Rabbi Judah HaNasi in 200 C.E. and to individual segments within that compilation.

Mitzvah: Commandment. A deed that one must perform or an action one must refrain from doing that is derived from the Torah or from a dictate of the rabbis.

Musaf: Addition. The additional public sacrifices brought on Shabbat, the new moon, and festivals when the Temple stood. Also, the name of the extra service recited on days when this sacrifice would have been brought.

Nasi: Exalted. The president of the Great Sanhedrin during the period of the *zugot*.

Nechemtah/Nechemtot: A message of comfort and hope that concludes prayers and sections of Talmud. These often make mention of the exodus from Egypt, the preeminent example of redemption.

Niddah/Niddot: A menstruating woman, who is therefore in a state of ritual impurity. It is forbidden to have sexual relations with a *niddah* until she has purified herself.

Olam HaBah: The world to come. The pleasant realm in the afterlife where the righteous are rewarded.

Ol Malchut Shamayim: "The yoke of the kingship of heaven." The first paragraph of the *Shema*, Deuteronomy 6:4–9.

Ol Mitzvot: "The yoke of the mitzvot." The second paragraph of the *Shema*, Deuteronomy 11:13–21.

Onein/Onenet: A person in the stage of mourning that extends from the moment of death until the burial is completed.

Pesach: "To pass over." The festival in the spring that celebrates the exodus from Egypt. This holiday marks the end of winter.

Pesachim: The tractate of the Babylonian Talmud that outlines the details of observance for the holiday of Pesach.

Peshat: The simple meaning of a verse or text.

Pirkei Avot: "Sayings of the fathers." A tractate of the Mishnah that outlines the ethical teachings of many sages.

Rosh HaShanah: "The head of the year." The Jewish new year, which occurs in the autumn. It is a time of judgment and repentance.

Saboraim (Stamaim): "The explainers." The sages of the period after the close of the Talmud (after 500). David Weiss Halivni (1986) calls them *Stamaim*, "the silent ones." Their opinions are not voiced explicitly in the Talmud, but they had great power over its contents, for they helped shape its final form.

Sandal: Miscarriage.

Sanhedrin: The court of seventy-one judges that was Israel's highest legislative and religious body. It met in the Temple courtyard.

Scriptures: The Torah, Prophets, and Writings. Torah is considered to be divinely revealed in traditional Judaism. Prophets and Writings have a lower level of holiness and authority.

Shabbat: The seventh day of the week. A day of rest that lasts from Friday sundown to Saturday sundown.

Shacharit: "Morning." The morning service; particularly the morning recitation of the *Shema* and *Amidah*.

Shema: "Hear." The central creed of Judaism. Consists of Deuteronomy 6:4–9, Deuteronomy 11:13–21, and Numbers 15:37–41. The first line must be said with intention.

Shemoneh Esrei: "Eighteen." Another name for the *Amidah*, the prayer par excellence.

Shelichot Tsibbur: "Messengers of the community," here in the plural, feminine form. One who may lead the community in prayer.

Shoresh: Root. The three-letter core of each Hebrew word.

Sugya/Sugyot: A talmudic discussion. Steinsaltz (1989) notes that this word is derived from the verb for "to go" in Aramaic. Thus a *sugya* literally means "walking" or "passage" (p. 77).

Sukkot: The harvest festival of the autumn. With this festival prayers for rain and the winter season commence (see Chapter 4).

Tadir/Sh'eino Tadir: "Regularly/not regularly." A factor concerning ranking or ordering of *mitzvot*, prayers, and the like, determined according to which comes more frequently. That which comes more frequently generally takes precedence over that which happens less frequently.

Tahara: The state of ritual purity; a kind of holiness. Opposite of *tumah*.

Tahor: The adjectival form of *tahara*. Ritually pure. Opposite of *tamei*.

Tallit: The garment that has the *tsitsit* tied to its four corners and is worn during prayer. (When the *tsitsit* are worn all day long, under one's clothes, they are attached to a garment called *arbah canfot*, "the four corners."

Tamei: The adjectival form of *tumah*; ritually impure. Opposite of *tahor*.

Tanach: The Hebrew acronym for the Scriptures. *Torah, Neviim* (Prophets), and *Ketuvim* (Writings).

Tanna/Tannaim: A teacher of the Oral Law. The *Tannaim* are the sages of the Mishnaic period, 10–220 C.E.

Tefillah/Tefillin: Phylacteries. Cube-shaped leather boxes that are tied to the hand and head during prayer. They contain the following passages written on parchment: Deuteronomy 6:4–9, Deuteronomy 11:13–21, Exodus 13:1–10, and Exodus 13:11–16.

Tefillah/Tefillot: Prayer/Prayers. Another name for the *Amidah* or *Shemoneh Esrei*. The prayer par excellence, which is said three times each day.

Terumah: The offering whose basis is Deuteronomy 18:4 and Numbers 18:12. This is an offering given to the priests from one's produce. It could be anywhere from one-fortieth to one-sixtieth of the total amount.

Teshuvah: Literally, "turning." Repentance.

Tevel: Food from which the tithes have not been separated out.

Torah: The first five books of the Bible: Genesis, Exodus, Leviticus, Numbers, and Deuteronomy. Also denotes Jewish learning in general.

Toraitic: From, or derived from, the first five books of the *Tanach*.

Tosefta/Toseftot: Literally, addition or supplement. Tannaitic material collected into a compendium. *Toseftot* do not have the authoritative stature of Mishnayot.

Tractate: A volume of the Talmud.

Tsedakah: Literally, justice or righteousness. Charity.

Tsitsit: The fringes attached to our garments to remind us to do the *mitzvot*. They are mentioned in the third paragraph of the *Shema*, Numbers 15:37–41.

Tumah: Ritual impurity. Opposite of *tahara*.

V'Ahavtah: "And you shall love." The first word of the first paragraph of the *Shema*, Deuteronomy 6:5–9.

Vocalize/Vocalization: The addition of vowels to a Hebrew or Aramaic text. Scriptures and Talmud were written without vowels.

Yerushalmi: "The Jerusalem one." The Talmud composed in the Land of Israel.

Yisurim shel Ahavah: "Afflictions of Love." The trials and pain that God sends to the righteous in this life so that they may overcome them and so earn a greater reward in the world to come; an explanation of why the righteous suffer.

Zimmun: The invitation to say grace that precedes *Birkat HaMazon*.

Zug/Zugot: Literally, "pair/pairs." The pairs of leaders that presided over the Sanhedrin. The pair consisted of the *nasi* (president) and *av beit din* (vice president). The era of the *zugot* lasted from approximately 175 B.C.E. to 10 C.E.

Zuz: A coin.

For Further Reading

Biale, R. (1984). *Women and Jewish Law: An Exploration of Women's Issues in Halakhic Sources*. New York: Schocken Books.
A thorough and easy-to-read exploration of women's roles in the Jewish tradition.

Blackman, P. (1977). *Mishnayoth*. Gateshead: Judaica Press.
The mishnah with vocalized Hebrew text, English translation and notes. A useful tool for the beginning student.

Blau, M. (1963). *Sefer Zichron Shalom Al Masechet Berachot. (Jerusalem)*. A commentary on *Berachot* in Hebrew.

Carmell, A. (1980). *Aids to Talmud Study*. New York: Feldheim.
A useful reference work for beginning Talmud scholars.

Encyclopedia Judaica (1972). Jerusalem: Keter.

Ehrman, A., (1982). *El Am Talmud, with English Translation and Commentary*. Jerusalem: El-Am, Hoza'a Leor Yisrael.
A wonderful commentary on this tractate, with extensive explanations and historical and cultural background.

Ginzberg, L. (1955). *On Jewish Law and Lore*. Philadelphia: Jewish Publication Society.
A very well written, insightful look at the development of Jewish law and the impact of economic and political events.

Guttman, A. (1970). *Rabbinic Judaism in the Making*. Detroit: Wayne State University Press.
A thorough historical overview of the founding of rabbinic Judaism. Good contrast to Ginzberg's point of view.

Halivni, D. (1986). *Midrash, Mishnah, and Gemara: The Jewish Predilection for Justified Law*. Cambridge, MA: Harvard University Press.

195

Halivni is a great modern scholar of the Talmud. This book is somewhat technical, but worth reading.

Harris, L. (1985). *Holy Days: The World of a Hasidic Family*. New York: Macmillan.
A marvelous book describing traditional Jewish life.

Heilman, S. (1984). *The Gate Behind the Wall: A Pilgrimage to Jerusalem*. New York: Summit.
A book about the spiritual power of Talmud study.

Herford, R. T. (1903). *Christianity in Talmud and Midrash*. New York: Ktav.
A reference work.

Hoffman, L. (1979). *The Canonization of the Synagogue Service*. Indiana: University of Notre Dame Press.
A technical, but interesting, survey of how the synagogue service developed.

—— (1989). *Beyond the Text: A Holistic Approach to Liturgy*. Indianapolis: Indiana University Press.
Hoffman helps the reader see the person behind the prayer.

Hyman, A. (1910). *Toledot Tanna'im ve-Amora'im*. (1964)
The classic reference work in Hebrew describing the sages.

Idelsohn, A. Z. (1932). *Jewish Liturgy and Its Development*. New York: Schocken.
A rather technical reference work.

Jastrow, M. (1903). *A Dictionary of the Targumim, the Talmud Bavli and Yerushalmi, and the Midrashic Literature*. Israel.
A dictionary for those reading the Talmud in the original.

Jonas, H. (1958). *The Gnostic Religion*. Boston: Beacon Press.
A description of Gnosticism, particularly in relation to Christianity.

Mielziner, M. (1968). *Introduction to the Talmud*. New York: Bloch.
A good, basic reference work on the Talmud.

Neusner, J. (1973). *Invitation to the Talmud: A Teaching Book*. New York: Harper & Row.
A book for the beginning Talmud student. Examines the eighth chapter of this tractate in depth.

Potok, C. (1967). *The Chosen*. New York: Random House.
A fictional work that gives some insight into the world of Talmud study.

Rivkin, E. (1971). *The Shaping of Jewish History: A Radical New Interpretation*. New York: Scribner's.
A wonderful conception of Jewish history.

Schurer, E. (1884). *The History of the Jewish People in the Age of Jesus Christ (75 B.C.–135 A.D.)* (1986) ed. Geza Vermes, Edinburgh: T & T Clark.
Good historical background on this period; particularly detailed descriptions of the Second Temple.

Seltzer, R. M. (1980). *Jewish People, Jewish Thought: The Jewish Experience in History*. New York: Macmillan.
An excellent resource. A general history of Jewish life and thought.

Simon, M. (1948). *Tractate Berakoth*. London: Soncino Press.
Translation of the Babylonian Talmud into English.

Steinsaltz, A. (1976). *The Essential Talmud*. New York: Basic Books.
Steinsaltz is one of the greatest teachers of Talmud in this millennium.

—— (1983). *Talmud Bavli, Tractate Berachot*. Jerusalem: Israel Institute for Talmudic Publications.
Steinsaltz's translation of *Berachot* into modern Hebrew. An indispensable study tool.

—— (1989). *The Talmud: The Steinsaltz Edition. A Reference Guide*. New York: Random House.
A guide to the historical background, methodology, and terminology used in Talmud study.

Strack, H. L. (1978). *Introduction to the Talmud and Midrash*. New York: Atheneum.
A technical reference work with many useful definitions and lists.

Teutsch, D. A. ed. (1989). *Kol Haneshama, Shabbat Eve*. Wyncote, PA: Reconstructionist Press.
The new Reconstructionist prayer book. Filled with beautiful poems, readings, and insights into Jewish prayer.

Yentl, a film based on the book by I. B. Singer, starring Barbra Streisand, gives a good account of what Talmud study used to be like in the last century.

Index

About the Author

Judith Abrams is the rabbi of Congregation Beth El in Missouri City, Texas. A member of the Central Conference of American Rabbis Responsa Committee, she is the author of *The Talmud for Beginners, Volume I: Prayer, The Talmud for Beginners, Volume II: Text,* and several prayer books for children.